COBOL PROGRAMMERS SWING WITH JAVA

In the fast-moving world of information technology, Java is now the #1 programming language. Programmers and developers everywhere need to know Java to keep pace with traditional and web-based application development. *COBOL Programmers Swing with Java* provides COBOL programmers a clear, easy transition to Java programming by drawing on the numerous similarities between COBOL and Java.

The authors introduce the COBOL programmer to the history of Java and object-oriented (OO) programming and then dive into the details of Java syntax, always contrasting it with the parallels in COBOL. A running case study gives the reader an overall view of application development with Java, with increased functionality as new material is presented. This second edition of the acclaimed *Java for the COBOL Programmer* features the development of graphical user interfaces (GUIs) using the latest in Java Swing components.

The clear writing style and excellent examples make the book suitable for anyone wanting to learn Java and OO programming, whether or not they have a background in COBOL.

E. Reed Doke is Professor Emeritus of Information Systems at Southwest Missouri State University in Springfield. He received his Ph.D. in Management and Computer Information Systems from the University of Arkansas. He worked for several years as a software developer and information systems manager prior to joining academia and continues to assist firms with systems development problems. He has published eight books and numerous articles focusing on object-oriented software development.

Bill C. Hardgrave is Associate Professor of Information Systems and Executive Director of the Information Technology Research Center, and he holds the Edwin & Karlee Bradberry Chair at the University of Arkansas. Prior to entering academia, he worked as a programmer, systems analyst, and general manager for two software development firms. He continues to help companies solve a variety of information systems–related problems. Dr. Hardgrave has published two books and more than 50 articles, primarily on the topic of software development.

Richard A. Johnson worked for several Fortune 500 companies as an industrial engineer and manager before receiving a Ph.D. in Computer Information Systems from the University of Arkansas in 1998. Since then, Dr. Johnson has published a text on systems analysis and design and fourteen articles in refereed journals. He is currently an Associate Professor of Computer Information Systems at Southwest Missouri State University, where he teaches Java programming and web application development.

COBOL PROGRAMMERS
SWING WITH JAVA

E. REED DOKE
Southwest Missouri State University

BILL C. HARDGRAVE
University of Arkansas

RICHARD A. JOHNSON
Southwest Missouri State University

CAMBRIDGE
UNIVERSITY PRESS

CAMBRIDGE
UNIVERSITY PRESS

Shaftesbury Road, Cambridge CB2 8EA, United Kingdom

One Liberty Plaza, 20th Floor, New York, NY 10006, USA

477 Williamstown Road, Port Melbourne, VIC 3207, Australia

314–321, 3rd Floor, Plot 3, Splendor Forum, Jasola District Centre, New Delhi – 110025, India

103 Penang Road, #05–06/07, Visioncrest Commercial, Singapore 238467

Cambridge University Press is part of Cambridge University Press & Assessment,
a department of the University of Cambridge.

We share the University's mission to contribute to society through the pursuit of
education, learning and research at the highest international levels of excellence.

www.cambridge.org
Information on this title: www.cambridge.org/9780521546843

First published 2005

A catalogue record for this publication is available from the British Library

Library of Congress Cataloging-in-Publication data
Doke, E. Reed.
COBOL programmers swing with Java / E. Reed Doke, Bill C. Hardgrave, Richard A. Johnson.
    p.   cm.
    Includes bibliographical references and index.
    ISBN 0-521-54684-2 (alk. paper)
    1. Java (Computer program language)   2. COBOL (Computer program language)
    I. Hardgrave, Bill C.   II. Johnson, Richard A. (Richard Allen), 1953 –   III. Title.
    QA76.73.J38D645   2004
    005.13'3 – dc22   2004048885

ISBN   978-0-521-54684-3   Paperback

"To Graham Reed Doke"

–Reed

"To Ronda, Rachel, and Gavin"

–Bill

"To Deborah and our children"

–Richard

Contents

Chapter 9
Data Access   173

Chapter 10
Graphical User Interfaces   197

Preface

If you are like most other programmers, you have probably been thinking about updating your technical skills. You have been hearing a lot about Java, object-oriented development, and Internet applications. These topics have been getting a tremendous amount of press lately. In the fanfare, you may have heard someone suggest that COBOL programmers will be obsolete and can't possibly make the switch to OO. Can this possibly be true? We don't think so.

We wrote this book because we believe it is important that you learn Java and OO development. Although we don't claim learning a new programming language is a trivial task, the fact that you already know COBOL gives you a head start on learning Java. Don't let what others say bother you.

We work with COBOL as consultants for industry, in our classrooms, and as authors. However, we also work with Java and object-oriented development. From our perspective, we believe COBOL and Java are highly complementary development tools in the evolving computing environment. COBOL does a great job of processing and maintaining a firm's data. Java plays an equally important role of capturing and reporting data by connecting clients to the server across a variety of networked computers, with little concern about the specific hardware and operating systems involved.

Today's business environment is diverse. A single platform and/or single language cannot meet the needs of most organizations. The business environment is becoming one of interconnectivity, requiring many different organizations with many different computing environments to communicate. Perhaps your organization is moving in this direction. Has your manager inquired about your interests in client-server computing or Java? The fact that you are reading this suggests you have been thinking about your future. We urge you to learn Java. Learn Java, not as a replacement for COBOL, but to make yourself even more valuable and make an even greater contribution to your firm's computing projects. Plus, we find writing Java fun and we think you will too!

Many COBOL programmers are asking questions such as: What is Java? How does it differ from COBOL? How is it similar? What is the impact of Java on COBOL? What is OO? We wrote this book to answer these questions for you.

Can you learn Java? Of course you can. Java has only 52 reserved words. At last count, COBOL had more than 600! These numbers suggest the Java language set is much easier to learn and remember than many others, including COBOL – our experience with Java makes us believe this is true. Plus, although it is not immediately obvious, there are a lot of similarities between COBOL and Java. In fact, some of the statements are almost identical. We include a lot of Java code in the book, and for most of it we have the corresponding COBOL code. Finally, because you already know programming constructs, you need to learn only the new syntax. But, you must also learn OO concepts and about half a dozen OO terms. Although they are not particularly difficult to learn, without these concepts you will find it nearly impossible to learn Java. Therefore, before we get into programming statements, Chapter 2 explains OO for you in simple straightforward terms. In this latest edition, we bring you up-to-date on developing graphical user interfaces (GUIs) using the Java Swing package (Chapter 10) so you too can "swing" with Java.

Good luck, have fun,
and let us hear from you.

Reed   RDoke@walton.uark.edu
Bill   BHardgrave@walton.uark.edu
Richard   RichardJohnson@smsu.edu

ACKNOWLEDGMENTS

We thank all the people who assisted us in making this book a reality, especially Lauren Cowles, Senior Editor, Mathematics and Computer Science at Cambridge University Press, and Dr. Neil Marple for his astute and speedy technical review.

Introduction

We organized the chapters in this book to be read in sequence. However, each chapter begins with a clear statement of what we assume you know before reading the chapter, so you can jump around a little bit, depending on your background and experience. You can use the book as a reference and jump in anywhere once you have the fundamentals.

Chapter 1 presents reasons why you should learn Java and describes the many similarities between COBOL and Java.

Chapter 2 explains what OO is, and what it is not. OO terms and concepts are described using several everyday examples.

Chapter 3 describes the overall structure and format of a Java program. Several small programs are developed to show you how to create objects and call methods.

Chapter 4 shows you how to define Java data items and use them in a program. Java data definition is somewhat different than COBOL and these differences are clearly explained and demonstrated in the program examples.

Chapter 5 introduces Java computation and, again, several small programs are written to illustrate the ideas and concepts present. You will see that some Java computation is nearly identical to COBOL.

Chapter 6 illustrates how to use the Java decision-making statements. We develop programs using the Java if (sound familiar?) and the Java counterpart to the COBOL EVALUATE verb.

Chapter 7 describes how to write Java loops. As you will learn, Java looping is different from COBOL.

Chapter 8 shows you how to define and work with Java arrays, which are really the old COBOL tables with a more technical-sounding name. There are a lot of parallels between Java arrays and COBOL tables.

Chapter 9 explains how to access data in sequential files, relational databases, and networks. You will appreciate Java's approach to accessing relational databases using standard SQL statements.

Chapter 10 illustrates how to develop graphical user interfaces for user input and output using the Java Swing package. This is an interesting and important chapter, even though there are few COBOL similarities.

Chapter 11 discusses OO development in a broader context. Both software and hardware issues are explored. Three-tier software design is illustrated using a GUI front end and a relational database back end.

All code listings can be found on the Cambridge University Press web site: **http://publishing.cambridge.org/resources/0521546842/**

CHAPTER 1

Why You Should Learn Java

OBJECTIVES

In this chapter you will study the following:

- An overview and history of Java;
- Some unique characteristics of Java;
- Reasons for learning Java; and
- An overview of the book

So, you want to learn Java. Why? You probably want to for one or all of the following reasons:

- As a COBOL programmer you feel a need to update your skills;
- Java is hot and so are the jobs for Java programmers;
- Object technology is hot and Java fits perfectly with the object-oriented development your boss is requiring you to learn; and
- You are a naturally curious person who wants to see what this Java stuff is all about.

Whatever your reasons, we're glad you're here!

In this book, we place the emphasis on learning Java from a COBOL perspective. Of the several million COBOL programmers worldwide, a significant number are, or soon will be, learning Java. We have designed this book to help you with that task. We will take what you know about COBOL and apply as much of it as possible to learning Java. But first, let's learn a little about Java in general, nontechnical terms and about object-oriented development. Chapters 1 and 2, respectively, have been set aside for these purposes.

This chapter covers a general survey of Java and the layout of the book. Our purpose is to present a brief history of Java, give you an overview of the language, describe why Java is becoming so popular, and discuss its impact on the future of COBOL.

Java is a relatively young language (circa 1995) and its explosive popularity demonstrates that it is rapidly becoming the language of choice for many firms. In fact, Java technology is being used by 100% of the Fortune 500 companies. Three main forces support Java's popularity in information systems today:

- The need to increase developer productivity;
- The adoption of the client-server model; and
- The growing number of Internet applications.

Java has received a lot of attention because it can be embedded in web pages to do input-output and animation. Java, however, offers much more. It is a complete, industrial-strength, full-featured application development language. It is also object-oriented, which facilitates implementation of the client-server model and Internet applications, plus it can significantly improve your productivity in developing all kinds of applications.

On the surface, Java appears to be a totally different language than COBOL. The reason is that Java is object-oriented and uses a much more concise (some say cryptic) syntax than COBOL. However, Java has numerous similarities with COBOL that can be used to enhance your learning process and ease the transition from COBOL to Java. It is much easier to learn a new concept (Java), when you can base it on something you already know (COBOL). That is precisely the premise of this book. We describe Java features and syntax in light of similar features and syntax that you already know in COBOL.

HISTORY AND OVERVIEW OF JAVA

Sun Microsystems, the creator of the Java programming language, says the following about Java technology:

The Java platform is the ideal platform for network computing. Running across all platforms—from servers to cell phones to smart cards—Java technology unifies business infrastructure to create a seamless, secure, networked platform for your business.

The Java platform benefits from a massive community of developers and supporters that actively work on delivering Java technology-based products and services as well as evolving the platform through an open, community-based, standards organization known as the Java Community Process program.

You can find Java technology in cell phones, on laptop computers, on the Internet, and even trackside at Formula One Grand Prix races. The fact is today, you can find Java technology just about everywhere!

Business Benefits:

- A richer user experience—Whether you're using a Java technology-enabled mobile phone to play a game or to access your company's network, the Java platform provides the foundation for true mobility. The unique blend of mobility and security in Java technology makes it the ideal development and deployment vehicle for mobile and wireless solutions.
- The ideal execution environment for Internet services—The Java and XML languages are the two most extensible and widely accepted computing languages on the planet, providing maximum reach to everyone, everywhere, every time, to every device and platform.
- Enabling business from end to end—Java offers a single, unifying programming model that can connect all elements of a business infrastructure.

Enough said? Such statements certainly tout many of the benefits of Java, but they don't say much about what it really is. Perhaps we should start with a brief history of Java.

Java began in the early 1990s as a project at Sun Microsystems. The idea was to create a language to support the development of systems embedded in consumer electronic devices. The project, headed by James Gosling, produced a language originally called Oak (named for the tree outside Gosling's window). Unknown at the time, another language had already taken the Oak name. The name was later changed from Oak to Java (the idea for the new name was generated during a visit to a local coffee shop).

C and C++ were available at the time and widely used. However, Sun was concerned about many of the complexities of the popular C++ language. Java is similar to C++, but avoids many of its problems.

After a few years and many changes, the Java language was redirected to the Internet. Fueled by the rapid growth of the Internet and Internet applications, Sun officially introduced Java in May 1995. Although Java initially gained recognition and acceptance because of its application to the Internet, it has mushroomed to a full-blown development language capable of producing mission critical systems on a wide range of hardware and operating systems.

The Java name is trademarked by Sun Microsystems, making it a commercial proprietary product. However, Java is in the public domain and a Java compiler can be obtained from Sun free of charge. Sun has been restrictive in its official licensing of the Java name to assure developers that anything bearing the Java seal meets the language standards and will run reliably in their environment.

During its brief history, Java has created a large following of software developers (some three million at last count) and a corresponding vocabulary. Many of the commonly used Java terms are listed in Table 1.1.

NOTES

1. You may visit Sun Microsystems at http://www.sun.com
2. A glossary of Java and related terms is available at http://java.sun.com/docs/glossary.html
3. The complete Java Language Specification is available at http://java.sun.com/docs/books/jls/second_edition/html/j.title.doc.html
4. The Java Language Environment: A White Paper is available at http://java.sun.com/docs/white/langenv/

THE POPULARITY OF JAVA

The popularity of Java is evident. Look at the number of Java books available (including this one!). You cannot pick up an industry newspaper or magazine (such as ComputerWorld© or InfoWorld©) without seeing numerous Java-related items. Java seems to be everywhere or, at least, everyone is talking about it. In March 1998, the month following the release of version 1.1 of Sun's Java Development Kit, more than 220,000 copies were downloaded from Sun's Internet site. The next month, more than 8000 developers attended the JavaOne© conference. By 2003, more than 3 million developers had registered through Sun's Java Developer Connection Internet site and downloads of the Java Development Kit had reached 72 million.

TABLE 1.1. Some Common Java Terms and Their Meanings

Term	Meaning
Applet	A Java component that typically executes in a web browser, but can execute in a variety of other applications or devices that support the applet programming model.
Bean (i.e., Java Bean)	A reusable software component. Beans can be combined to create an application.
Bytecode	Machine-independent code generated by the Java compiler and executed by the Java interpreter.
Java ARchive files (JAR files)	A Java file format used for compressing many files into one to improve transmission speed across network connections.
Java Software Development Kit (SDK)	Sun's software development environment for writing applets and applications in the Java programming language.
Java Integrated Development Environment (IDE)	A complete Java development environment including text editors, compilers, debuggers, interpreters, etc.
JavaScript	A web scripting language that is used in both browsers and web servers. Like all scripting languages, it is used primarily to tie other components together or to accept user input.
Java virtual machine (JVM)	The Java interpreter, a software "execution engine" that safely and compatibly executes the bytecodes in Java class files on a microprocessor (whether in a computer or in another electronic device).
Servlet	Similar to an applet, but located on a server, a Java program that extends the functionality of a web server, generating dynamic content and interacting with web clients using a request-response paradigm.

But, is Java actually being used? The answer is an emphatic YES! According to the most recent JavaOne© conference in San Francisco (keying on the slogan, "Java Everywhere"):

• Seventy-eight percent of executives view Java technology as the best platform for Internet services (source: Giga, Computerworld);

- Java technology is installed and running in almost 550 million desktops; and
- Almost 74 percent of professional developers use the Java programming language as their primary development language, surpassing the 51 percent who use Visual Basic (source: IDC).

In higher education, the use of Java has also grown rapidly. Java's use in university curricula jumped from 0 percent in 1995 to 43 percent in 1998, and then to 90 percent in 2002—not bad for a language officially less than ten years old.

Will Java's meteoric growth continue? Only time will tell. Initially, the growth of Java mirrored the growth of the web as Java was primarily used as a tool for building applets. However, its recent growth is in the area of business applications. The popularity of the Java Software Development Kit (SDK) may be a sign of continued growth for Java in business applications.

In its short life, Java has grown faster and gained wider acceptance than any other language before. Why? Certainly, the growth of the web and Java applets initially fueled Java's popularity. However, Java offers many distinct advantages in application development not available in other languages. Let's take a closer look at how Java compares.

WHAT MAKES JAVA DIFFERENT?

Java is just another programming language, right? Yes, it is another programming language, but it is also much more. Some would say the language is simple. For example, Java has only 48 reserved words. At last count, COBOL had over 600! These numbers suggest the language set for Java is much easier to learn and remember than many others, including COBOL—our experience with Java makes us believe this is true.

Java is purely object-oriented, which puts it in select company (along with other pure object-oriented languages such as Smalltalk and Eiffel). Java is also portable, enabling it to run on many different platforms. These factors (and others) combine to create an environment of improved development productivity and programming excellence. Let's explore further the issues of simplicity, object-orientation, and portability.

Java Is Simple

Java really is simple, especially if you know C++, which Java closely resembles. Is it simpler than COBOL? Is it more difficult than Smalltalk? The answers to these questions vary by individual. However, it is probably safe to say that Java is easier to learn than C++ but more difficult than Basic. How's that for a wide range? Our goal in this book is to make Java simple for you, the COBOL programmer. We think you will quickly conclude that Java is certainly no more difficult than COBOL to use, and that you will come to appreciate and even prefer its syntax.

Remember the history of Java: Gosling's group at Sun took C++ as the foundation and eliminated many of its problems. The Eiffel, Smalltalk, and Objective-C languages, among others, also influenced Java. Starting with C++, the troublesome features such as operator overloading, multiple inheritance, and pointers were removed. Features absent in C++, such as automatic garbage collection and memory management, were added. Overall, Java developers added some of the best and removed some of the worst features of several popular languages.

Java Is Object-Oriented

Java is a *pure* object-oriented language. *Pure* means that everything is represented as an object and all of the major characteristics of object-orientation such as inheritance, classes, and polymorphism are supported (the next chapter explores the details of object-orientation). Smalltalk and Eiffel are examples of other pure OO languages.

In Java, everything is an object except primitive data types (we discuss these in Chapter 4). Single inheritance and polymorphism are supported. A *hybrid* language, on the other hand, uses an existing procedural language as its base and adds object-oriented features and syntax. For example, C++ (derived from C), Object COBOL (derived from COBOL), and Object Pascal (derived from Pascal), are all hybrid languages. In many cases, hybrid languages do not fully support all OO characteristics.

The motivation for hybrid languages is a shorter learning curve. Developers can use their familiar language as the base and simply learn the OO extensions. The danger, of course, is that developers do not truly learn OO development. Rather, they learn how to write procedural programs in an OO context. Java forces compliance to object-oriented development. With Java, it is difficult to revert back to procedural programming. However, the mere use of Java does not ensure a successful development project. Good analysis and design remain essential prerequisites to writing successful applications.

In the true spirit of OO, Java applications can be built by assembling JavaBeans in a Java Integrated Development Environment (IDE). In other words, JavaBeans (independent software components or objects) can be combined to form an application. For example, a customer object and bank account object can be combined to form a banking application. Reusable independent software components are the foundation of object-oriented development. Soon, you will be writing these components using Java and then assembling them into functioning software.

Java Is Portable

Portability is the ability to run an application on different platforms (hardware and software configurations) without making changes to the code. Many of us have experienced the problems associated with moving an application from one platform to another. Typically, it required identifying code that needed changing, then recompiling and testing every program in the application. Our task would have been trivial if our application had been portable.

With the multitude of platforms available, such as Windows 2000, Windows XP, Linux, and Solaris, portability is a very useful feature. Portability is, perhaps, Java's most appealing feature. In fact, "*write once, run anywhere*" is a common Java slogan.

What gives Java the portability that so many other languages lack? *Bytecode* and *Java virtual machines* (JVMs) are the keys. In most cases, when a program is compiled, machine code is created. For example, a COBOL program is compiled into machine code that can be executed directly by a computer. However, machine code is not portable across various platforms and must be created specifically for the platform to be used. A COBOL program that runs on UNIX probably will not run on MVS and most certainly will not execute on a Windows 2000 system. In the traditional *compiled* environment, multiple platforms mean multiple compilers, as illustrated in Figure 1.1. If I want my COBOL program to run on UNIX, MVS, and Windows 2000, I need a compiler for UNIX, MVS, and Windows 2000. Unfortunately, even with multiple compilers, there is no assurance that the source code will compile and run correctly across all the platforms.

Alternatively, Java source code is compiled into *bytecode*. Bytecode is not machine code, and therefore is not directly executable. Instead, bytecode is an intermediate format—somewhere between source code and machine code. For bytecode to be executed on a computer, another tool, called a *virtual machine* is needed to interpret the bytecodes. A Java virtual machine (JVM) is a program that interfaces with the local operating system and hardware. The

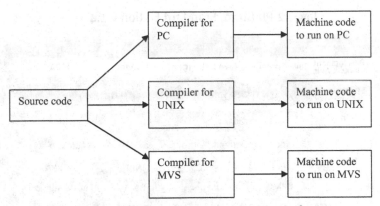

FIGURE 1.1. Multiple compilers for multiple platforms.

JVM interprets the bytecode at runtime so that the Java program can run on the local platform, as illustrated in Figure 1.2.

Many different JVMs exist to accommodate the many different platforms. Therefore, only one version of the bytecode file is needed to run on many platforms. Bytecodes are platform independent and portable *as long as a JVM is available for the platform for which you want to run the bytecodes*. The combination of bytecodes and JVM guarantees portability—no need to recompile the program for each platform, no need to have multiple compilers for multiple platforms.

Fortunately, many operating systems are providing JVMs for their environment. Currently, Windows 9x, Windows NT, Windows XP, Solaris, HP-UX, IRIX, AIW, and MacOS, among others, support Java. Also, Internet web browsers such as Netscape and Internet Explorer contain bytecode interpreters so that when a Java applet is recognized, it is interpreted and executed.

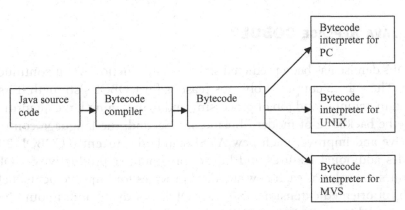

FIGURE 1.2. Java running on multiple platforms.

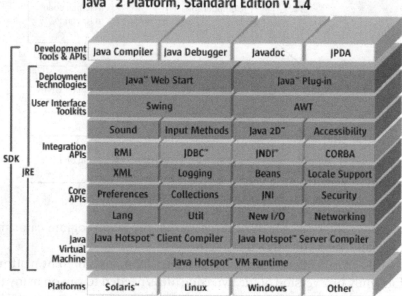

Source: http://java.sun.com/j2se/1.4.2/docs/index.html

FIGURE 1.3. Structure of the Java SDK.

However, as you probably have begun to suspect, interpreting a bytecode program is slower than executing native code for a particular platform. In situations where execution speed is vital, Java can be compiled into native code (Just like COBOL) and then it will run as fast as any other application language. To give you a general idea of how the different parts of the Java SDK work together to run applications on a variety of platforms, see Figure 1.3.

WILL JAVA REPLACE COBOL?

COBOL's demise has been predicted since its introduction, yet it continues to thrive. There are a couple of obvious reasons for COBOL's strength. First, it does an incredibly good job of processing and maintaining large quantities of data—the backbone of modern businesses. Second, the language continues to evolve and improve. Each new ANSI standard (currently COBOL 2002) provides additional features and boosts programmer productivity. COBOL continues to evolve as each new standard provides for improvements including object-oriented extensions. No, COBOL is not dying and, in our view, it isn't even sick!

There are more than 3 million COBOL programmers in the world. More than 70% of all code, representing as much as 225 billion lines, is written in COBOL. Will Java replace COBOL anytime soon? We doubt it. The year 2000 (Y2K) problem certainly rekindled the demand and interest in COBOL programming, but will such levels of interest continue into the future? You may have asked yourself this question. To set the record straight, the demand for COBOL programmers has been increasing for many years. Y2K projects may have caused a blip in the demand curve, but the shortage of COBOL people did not begin with Y2K cleanup efforts and will certainly not end as we continue to move into the new millennium. In fact, COBOL programmers are currently needed to maintain all the new COBOL code written for Y2K and to assist in enterprise application integration (EAI) efforts.

Bridging the gap between traditional COBOL development and the new world of e-business and web-enabled applications will be critical in the years to come. As a result, programmers who possess skills in COBOL and new programming languages, such as Java and XML (Extensible Markup Language, a flexible way to create common information formats and share both the format and the data on the World Wide Web, intranets, and elsewhere) are poised to take a lead role in major enterprise software projects.

Will Java replace COBOL as the primary development language in the long run? Several unanswered questions impact the long-term use of COBOL:

- Will OO development continue to be adopted by organizations? The increase, or decrease, in use of OO development in organizations will affect the use of object-oriented languages overall.
- Will Object COBOL be widely accepted? If Object COBOL is widely accepted as the next generation of COBOL, then a smooth migration path is provided to OO development. As such, companies may stick with COBOL (albeit Object COBOL) rather than switching to Java.
- What will happen to all those new COBOL programmers hired to deal with Y2K? Will these programmers continue to use COBOL, or will they move into a new area of programming, such as Java? Evidence suggests that these COBOL programmers are still needed to get legacy systems to work with new technologies such as the Web, and Java is a big part of that strategy.
- Will Microsoft continue to pursue its own language strategy to compete with Sun? Yes! In 2000, Microsoft launched the C# language, part of its .NET strategy, as an alternative to Java. The incompatibilities between the two groups could hinder Java's portability and ultimate widespread

TABLE 1.2. Primary Languages Taught in Undergraduate IS Programs

Language (alphabetically)	June 1995*	Feb. 1998*	Dec. 2002**
C	54.9%	26.4%	21.7%
C++	59.7%	52.8%	53.6%
COBOL	89.7%	52.8%	36.2%
Java	—	42.5%	90.0%
Visual Basic	59.1%	69.8%	90.0%
Other†	12.7%	11.3%	26.1%

*Source: Douglas and Hardgrave, 1998.
**Source: Internet Survey, 2002.
†Includes HTML, JavaScript, XML, ASP, Delphi, Assembly, VBA, C#, and Unix

acceptance, but this isn't likely. In fact, Microsoft and Sun reached a land-mark agreement in 2004 to enter into a broad technology collaboration arrangement to enable their products to work better together and to settle all pending litigation between the two companies..

One indication of Java's encroachment into COBOL's camp is the use of the two languages in higher education information systems curricula. During the period June 1995 (remember: Java was officially introduced in May 1995) to February 1998, the teaching of Java increased from 0 percent to nearly 43 percent of information systems programs of study. On the other hand, COBOL declined from 90 percent to less than 53 percent during the same time period (see Table 1.2). Let's say that again:

- Java increased from 0 to 43 percent; and
- COBOL decreased from 90 to 53 percent.

Because it is difficult to add a course to a curriculum without removing a course, one would expect that Java replaced COBOL in many college curricula in the mid to late 1990s. And the trend continues to the present day. Table 1.2 also demonstrates that Java has continued to grow in popularity within information systems curricula as penetration reaches 90 percent. On the other hand, COBOL has continued its slide to 36 percent. Figure 1.4 illustrates these trends graphically.

TABLE 1.3. Programming Languages Sought in Technical Job Offerings		
Language (alphabetically)	Number of Jobs	Percentage of Jobs
C or C++	1252	27.7%
C++ only	675	14.9%
COBOL	232	5.1%
Java	1532	33.9%
Visual Basic	829	18.3%
Total	4520	100.0%

Source: http://www.dice.com, July 8, 2003.

Another interesting perspective can be gained by exploring the number of programming jobs listed on nationwide job search web sites. A recent inquiry at http://www.dice.com revealed that while either C or C++ are certainly desirable development languages, Java is the single most popular and surpasses COBOL by a ratio of nearly 7 to 1 (see Table 1.3).

Why should COBOL programmers be retrained in Java? Why should YOU learn Java?

- COBOL programmers typically have a high-quality, zero-defect attitude. This type of attitude is needed to develop reusable objects that must be of high quality.
- COBOL programmers have a strong development process discipline. This discipline is needed in a Java OO development environment. Adherence to methodical analysis and design is crucial to the successful development of any complex system.

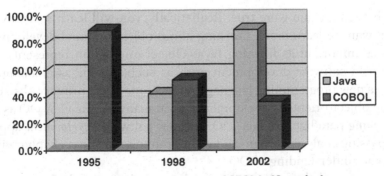

FIGURE 1.4. Popularity of Java vs. COBOL in IS curricula.

- COBOL programmers already know the business environment. COBOL programmers are familiar with important business issues and processes. This knowledge gives you an edge when developing Java applications.
- COBOL programmers already know programming. You already know the logic of the various programming structures: sequence, selection, and iteration. You only need to learn the new syntax.
- Knowing two languages gives you a sharper perspective when designing systems. You can see solutions that are not necessarily tied to a single language.

From our perspective, we don't see Java as COBOL's replacement. Instead, we believe COBOL and Java are complementary development tools in the evolving client-server environment. COBOL's job is to process and maintain the firm's data. Java plays a complementary role by capturing and reporting data by connecting the client to the server across a variety of networked computers, with little concern about the specific hardware and operating systems involved.

Today's business environment is diverse. A single platform and/or single language cannot meet the needs of most organizations. The business environment is becoming one of interconnectivity, requiring many different organizations with many different computing environments to communicate.

How to Use This Book

After reading this book, you will be the world's best object-oriented software developer!

We wish such a claim were true. Realistically, you will learn *some* Java, but you will want to learn more. Learning about object-oriented development is equally as important as learning Java. Object-orientation represents a new paradigm in software development and, as such, can be as challenging as learning a new programming language. In fact, one of the primary obstacles to adopting object-oriented development is that many people view OO as a new *programming* paradigm. In fact, OO is a new software *development* approach encompassing analysis, design, **and** programming. The next chapter will give you a good understanding of OO.

Our main goal throughout this book is to show you how to make the transition from COBOL to Java by using your existing COBOL knowledge. As

TABLE 1.4. A Comparison of COBOL and Java	
COBOL	Java
Arithmetic Operators	Arithmetic Operators
Boolean Operators	Boolean Operators
Calling Subprograms	Invoking Methods
Compute	Assignment
Conditions	Conditions
Evaluate Verb	Switch Statement
If-Then-Else	If-Then-Else
Intrinsic Functions	Class Library
Literals	Literals
Move	Assignment
Passing Arguments	Passing Arguments
Perform-Until	While
Perform-Until-Test After	Do—While
Perform-Varying	For Loop
Tables	Arrays

you progress through the various chapters of this book you will realize that nearly everything in Java can be compared to COBOL. Table 1.4 lists several examples.

There are several approaches to using the material in this book. One method is to read the book from the beginning to the end. This will give you an excellent overall understanding of Java and the similarities and differences between COBOL and Java.

However, the book can also be used as a reference by looking up only those things you need when you need them. For example, if you are interested in defining variables, then read Chapter 3. Or if you only want to know how to change variable data types, then see the section entitled "Changing Variable Data Types" in Chapter 3.

Each chapter will provide the necessary translation of COBOL to Java for the major programming components such as data definition, decision making, arithmetic operations, looping, tables and arrays, and input and output. Samples of COBOL code and corresponding Java code are provided to illustrate the similarities and differences between the two languages. All of our program code can be found at the Cambridge University Press web site, http://www.cup.com.

Overall, you will learn the basics of Java in this book. However, you will not learn all the details of the Java language. For example, we deliberately avoid building web-based Java applets for two reasons. First, COBOL has no counterpart; second and perhaps more importantly, numerous excellent books already deal with this topic. See the bibliography at the end of this chapter for more information.

Neither will you learn everything about developing OO software, especially OO analysis and design. Again, the focus here is moving from COBOL to Java and there are other excellent books on OO analysis and design. We encourage you to continue learning about OO development and the Java language before building critical applications.

We think you will find Java to be an easy language to learn despite what you might have heard. Your COBOL knowledge base and your programming experience will prove very useful in the transition.

Remember: understanding both COBOL and Java makes you a more valuable programming professional.

Good luck and have fun!

SUMMARY OF KEY POINTS IN CHAPTER 1

1. Java is a new language, originally created in the early 1990s and released in May 1995 by Sun Microsystems.
2. Java can do a lot more than make cute web page animations. It is a full-featured industrial-strength application development language.
3. Java is based on the C++ language, thus making it easy for C++ programmers to learn Java. Java removed the trouble-prone features of C++ and added some helpful tools.
4. Java is a pure object-oriented language, which means that everything, except primitive data types, is represented as an object. This means you need to know a little about OO before you can learn Java. Chapter 2 introduces you to OO. You will be surprised how simple it really is!
5. Java is portable. It can run on many different platforms without making changes to the code. A program called the Java compiler produces a byte-code file (an intermediate compiled code) and the Java virtual machine interprets the bytecode. Where execution speed is an issue, native Java code can be produced to bypass the interpretation process.
6. Many issues face Java in the near future. However, it appears to be poised to be one of the most popular programming languages.

7. There are many similarities between COBOL and Java, which will enhance and simplify your learning Java.

BIBLIOGRAPHY

Altendorf, E., Hohman, M., and Zabicki, R. (2002). "Using J2EE on a Large, Web-Based Project," *IEEE Software*, 19(2), 81–92.

Dietel, H. M., and Dietel, P. J. (2003). *Java: How to Program*, Upper Saddle River, NJ: Prentice Hall, 5th ed., 2003.

Doke, E. R., Satzinger, J. W., and Williams, S. R. (2002). *Object-Oriented Application Development Using Java*, Cambridge, MA: Course Technology. ISBN 0-619-03565-X.

Douglas, D. E., and Hardgrave, B. C. (1998). "The Changing Language Mix in Information Systems Curricula," in *1998 Proceedings of the National Decision Sciences Institute*, pp. 877–79.

Garside, R., and Mariani, J. (2002). *Java: First Contact*, 2nd Ed. Pacific Grove, CA: Brooks/Cole.

"Glossary of Java and Related Terms," available at *http://java.sun.com/docs/glossary.html*

Gosling, J., and McGilton, H., "The Java Language Environment: A White Paper," available at *http://java.sun.com/docs/white/langenv/*

Gosling, J., Joy, B., and Steele, G., The Java Language Specification, available at *http://java.sun.com/docs/books/jls/second_edition/html/j.title.doc.html*

Hardgrave, B., and Doke, E. (2000). "COBOL in an Object-Oriented World: A Learning Perspective," *IEEE Software*, 19(2), 26–29.

Nilsen, K. (1998). "Adding Real-Time Capabilities to Java," *Communications of the ACM*, 41(6), 49–56.

Pancake, C. M., and Lengauer, C. (2001). "High-Performance Java," *Communications of the ACM*, 44(10), 98.

Radding, A. (1997). "Tool Immaturity Tempers Java Buzz," *Software Magazine*, 17(8), 51–54.

Robins, A., Roundtree, J., and Roundtree, N. (2003). "Learning and Teaching Programming: A Review and Discussion," *Computer Science Education*, 13(2), 137–73.

Singhal, S., and Nguyen, B. (1998). "The Java Factor," *Communications of the ACM*, 41(6), 34–37.

"The Java Language: An Overview," available at _http://java.sun.com/docs/ overviews/java/java-overview-1.html_

Tyma, P. (1998). "Why Are We Using Java Again?" _Communications of the ACM_, 41(6), 38–42.

Udell, J. (2002). "Java, XML, and Web services," _InfoWorld_, 24(12), 52–54.

Vaughan-Nichols, S. J. (2003). "The Battle over the Universal Java IDE," _Computer_, 36(4), 21–24.

CHAPTER 2

An Introduction to Object-Oriented Programming

OBJECTIVES

In this chapter you will study:

- The history of OO;
- What it means to be object-oriented; and
- Key object-oriented concepts.

This chapter is devoted to the introduction of the key concepts essential to your understanding of the OO paradigm in general and writing OO code in particular. This chapter describes the primary OO concepts: *objects*, *classes*, *inheritance*, *encapsulation*, *polymorphism*, and *dynamic binding*. A basic understanding of these ideas will enable you to begin writing Java programs and developing object-oriented systems.

Several examples are used throughout the chapter to illustrate the concepts. In most cases, the examples are based on everyday things with which you are already familiar. A case study (The Community National Bank Case) is introduced at the beginning of the chapter and will be used to illustrate OO concepts. The case study will continue to be used throughout the remainder of the book.

NOTES

1. OO development is a *different way of thinking* about the development of systems—it is not simply a programming technique.
2. Although programming languages were the first to utilize the ideas of OO, the concepts of OO are prevalent throughout all phases of development—analysis, design, and programming.
3. It is very important that you understand the basics of OO before attempting to write a Java program.

The chapter assumes a basic understanding of computing and programming; it does not, however, assume a prior knowledge of object-oriented concepts.

THE COMMUNITY NATIONAL BANK

The Community National Bank (CNB) is a small, privately owned bank located in a medium-sized city in the Midwestern United States. The bank was established during the early 1900s and is owned and managed by the descendants of the founder. CNB offers the typical small bank services such as checking and savings accounts, certificates of deposit, safe deposit box rental, and loans.

Defying a nationwide trend, CNB remains independent and privately owned. The bank has nearly $200 million in deposits and 60 employees.

CNB takes advantage of its relatively small size by providing personalized attentive service to its customers, especially its small business accounts.

As you learn about OO and Java, we will develop software to provide processing for CNB and its customers.

HISTORY OF OO

With the recent growth in interest in OO development, you may think that OO represents a new set of ideas and concepts. On the contrary, OO is not new. In fact, the beginning of OO can be traced to the mid-1960s!

Many credit the beginning of OO to the introduction of Simula, a simulation language, developed by Dahl and Nygaard in 1966. The language was officially known at that time as Simula-67. Many of the core elements of today's OO languages were contained in this early language. Also during this period of time, a professor at the University of Utah, Alan Kay, was working on the FLEX system. His goal was to develop a computer that could be used by nonexperts. Simula was a guiding force for his work. A few years later, Kay headed the Dynabook project at the Xerox Palo Alto Research Center (PARC). The outcome of the project was some new hardware plus a new programming language named *Smalltalk*, the first object-oriented programming language (OOPL). In fact, Kay is credited with coining the terms "object-oriented" and "object-oriented programming." Smalltalk was officially released in 1972 and remains in use today.

After Smalltalk's introduction, several years passed before object-oriented programming received widespread attention. During the mid-1980s, new object-oriented languages such as Objective-C, Eiffel, Flavors, and C++ were introduced. Some of the languages, such as Eiffel, were *pure* object-oriented languages; others, such as C++, were *hybrids*. Pure OO languages view everything as an object and encompass the OO concepts to be discussed later in the chapter. Hybrid languages are a modification of an existing language with OO capabilities. One advantage of the hybrid languages is the short learning curve. For example, C++ quickly found a large following due in large part to the popularity of its immediate predecessor, the C language. In 1996, early versions of Object COBOL, another hybrid language, were released.

In May 1995, Sun Microsystems introduced Java, another pure OOPL. Perhaps no other programming language in history has witnessed the tremendous amount of attention and subsequent use that Java has experienced. Fueled by its web applications and client-server architecture, Java has exploded onto the programming scene. Many believe Java will be the next COBOL of programming languages. As you will see, Java is a very powerful language.

In addition to the proliferation of OOPL introductions in the mid-1980s, OO analysis and design methods began to appear. Led by the design method developed by Grady Booch, largely from his work with the Ada programming language, a plethora of methods appeared, such as Objectory, OMT, Shlaer/Mellor, and Coad/Yourdon, among others. This was both good news and bad news for the software development industry. It was good because OO was beginning to receive increased attention by researchers, academicians, and industry leaders and several methods were emerging to assist in the development of OO systems. It was bad because the methods were very different, employing different approaches and notation. This divergence of methods and notation sets undoubtedly slowed the adoption of OO. In response to this confusion, the Unified Modeling Language (UML) was adopted by the Object Management Group (OMG) as a standard notation set and metamodel for OO modeling in 1997. UML represents the efforts of many different individuals and organizations, but it is primarily based on the prior work of Grady Booch, Jim Rumbaugh, and Ivar Jacobson. The adoption of a standard should help ease the burden of adopting organizations. This book uses UML notation.

With a standard notation set, the future will focus on the establishment of a standard development methodology that will utilize UML, a set of standards for object-oriented databases, and OO CASE tools to support software development. Programming languages will always be an issue, but it appears that a few languages, particularly Java, will be dominant.

OBJECTS

Look around you—you probably see familiar items such as chairs, tables, books, and pencils. Could you describe these items to a person such that they would understand what you are describing? If you close your eyes and someone hands you a pencil, could you determine the item without looking? The answer to both is (hopefully) yes. Let's think about how you would describe, for example, a pencil. One might say that the item is about six inches long, wooden, round, sharp on one end, and dull on one end; it can write and it can erase. By describing the item (in this case, a pencil), data *about* the item (length, material, etc.) and descriptions of what the item *can do* (write and erase) are used. In OO terminology, you have described an *object*. An object contains both data (what it knows about itself) and behavior (what it can do). In this case, the pencil knows its length, material, shape, and ends; and it can write and erase. In OO parlance, the things an object knows about itself are called *attributes*; the things it can do are called *methods*. Thus, an object can be defined as data (attributes) and a set of behaviors (methods).

In object-oriented programming, we write software that models real world objects. Real world objects can be tangible things such as a car, an airplane, a computer, and a person, or less tangible such as a transaction. The Community National Bank system will have numerous objects such as customer, employee, and account. Can you think of some attributes and methods for each of these objects?

Attributes for a CheckingAccount object would certainly include *accountNumber* and *balance*. Methods may include **computeServiceCharge()**

and **recordACheck()**. A specific CheckingAccount object might be called aCheckingAccount or myCheckingAccount. For these elements, we use the following notation:

1. Class names: underlined, mixed case with the first letter of each word capitalized, no spaces or hyphens. Example: CheckingAccount.
2. Attribute names: italicized, mixed case with the first letter lowercase, first letter of remaining words capitalized, no spaces or hyphens.
   Example: *accountNumber*.
3. Method names: boldface, mixed case, the first letter lowercase, first letter of remaining words capitalized, no spaces or hyphens, begins with a verb (since we are using the Java language, it is customary to include a set of parentheses with the method name).
   Example: **recordACheck()**.
4. Object names: based on class name (denoting a specific instance of the class), first letter not capitalized, first letter of remaining words capitalized, no spaces or hyphens, not underlined.
   Example: aCheckingAccount.

CLASSES

A *class* is a group of objects that share common attributes and common methods. Referring to our earlier pencil example, we could have a drawer full of pencils of various colors, shapes, and sizes. Although different, each would be considered a pencil. They would all have a length, a shape, and could write and erase. However, the values of those attributes would vary depending on the pencil. For example, one pencil could be 6 inches long, plastic, square, use #2 lead, and have a big eraser, while another pencil might be 8 inches long, wooden, round, use #3 lead, and have a small eraser. Both of these are still considered pencils because they belong to the class of pencils—they share common attributes and methods. It is the value of the attributes and the way in which the methods (behaviors) are conducted that differentiate members of the class, and allows us to identify particular pencil objects. Think of a class as the epitome of all objects in the class; it describes a collection of objects, or an object type, but not any one particular object (i.e., it lacks sufficient detail, such as values of attributes and details of the behaviors).

In the next chapter, we will write a Java program to describe the attributes and methods of a class. This program is called a *class program*. For the

Community National Bank system we will write class programs to represent Account, Customer, and others.

Java refers to specific objects as *instances*. In developing the CNB system, we will write a class program to define and describe Account. Specific accounts are called Account instances or objects. We will actually have one object for each account at CNB. If the bank has 5,000 accounts, then there will be 5,000 objects of the account class, but we will have only one account class. Remember the actual data (account number and balance) reside in the object, but the *description* of the data is defined in the class program.

You should also be aware that the definitions of class, object, and instances are not universal and, unfortunately, they vary by the OO method or the OO language utilized. For example, some use the terms instance and object interchangeably. Here we follow the definitions that correspond to the way in which they are used by the Java language.

DIAGRAMMING CLASSES AND OBJECTS

Throughout this book, the Unified Modeling Language (UML) notation will be used where appropriate. Figure 2.1 illustrates the UML notation for a class. Note that it has three sections: the name of the class, its attributes, and its methods. Here we italicize attribute names and bold method names.

We also use UML to diagram an object as shown in Figure 2.2. The name aPencil is called the object name or object pointer. We will develop this idea in much more detail in the next chapter. The pencil (object) is 6 inches long, is made of wood, is round, has an eraser on one end and lead on the other

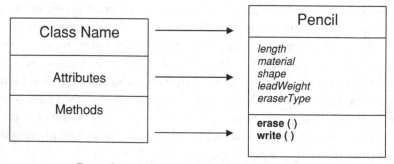

FIGURE 2.1. A class symbol using UML notation.

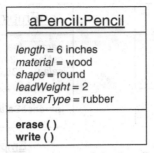

FIGURE 2.2. An object of the <u>Pencil</u> class.

end, can write, and can erase. This particular pencil (object) belongs to the class of all pencils.

Figure 2.3 provides another example. aDog is an object with name Fido. aDog weighs 20 pounds, is 15 inches tall, can bark, and can bite. aDog belongs to the class <u>Dog</u>.

According to Figure 2.4, anEmployee is an object with name Joe. anEmployee has an SSN of 123-45-6789 and a salary of $35,000; he can increase his salary (by earning a raise).

The Community National Bank system has several classes, as shown in Figure 2.5.

Understanding OO analysis and design will enhance your OO programming. Unlike structured development where design is separate from programming, OO programming, OO analysis, and OO design are well integrated. This book focuses on OO programming and will enable you to begin writing OO programs using Java; but to really understand OO, you should investigate OO analysis and design. There are many excellent books on the subject and several are listed at the end of this chapter.

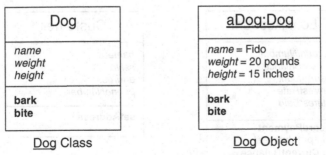

FIGURE 2.3. A <u>Dog</u> class and object.

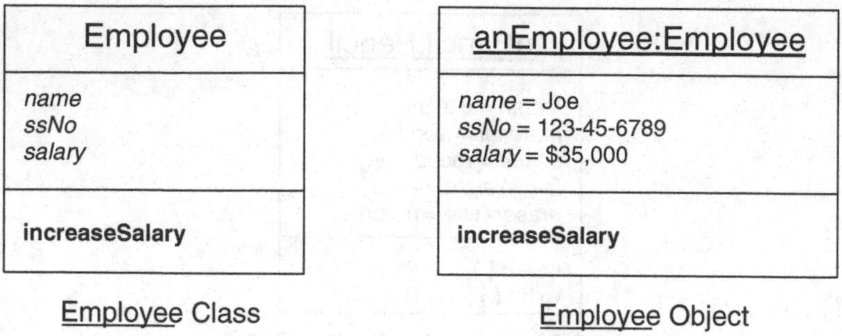

Employee	anEmployee:Employee
name *ssNo* *salary*	*name* = Joe *ssNo* = 123-45-6789 *salary* = $35,000
increaseSalary	**increaseSalary**

<u>Employee</u> Class   <u>Employee</u> Object

FIGURE 2.4. An <u>Employee</u> class and object.

CLASS RELATIONSHIPS

In object-orientation there are three distinguishable types of relationships:

1. Inheritance
2. Aggregation
3. Association

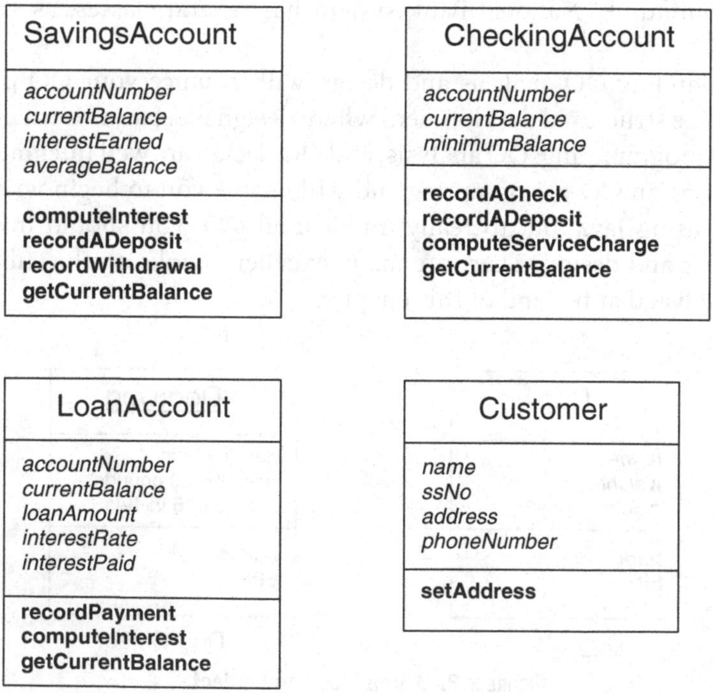

SavingsAccount
accountNumber *currentBalance* *interestEarned* *averageBalance*
computeInterest **recordADeposit** **recordWithdrawal** **getCurrentBalance**

CheckingAccount
accountNumber *currentBalance* *minimumBalance*
recordACheck **recordADeposit** **computeServiceCharge** **getCurrentBalance**

LoanAccount
accountNumber *currentBalance* *loanAmount* *interestRate* *interestPaid*
recordPayment **computeInterest** **getCurrentBalance**

Customer
name *ssNo* *address* *phoneNumber*
setAddress

FIGURE 2.5. Community National Bank classes.

The *inheritance* relationship, also known as the IS-A or generalization/specialization relationship (gen-spec for short), is appropriate for those situations where one class needs to share attributes or behaviors with other classes. *Aggregation*, also referred to as HAS-A, CONSISTS-OF, and PART-WHOLE, is used to illustrate a relationship among classes where one class is a component or part of another class. An *association* is a relationship between classes that is not inheritance or aggregation, but rather a general linkage between classes.

INHERITANCE

Inheritance is a relationship among classes wherein one class shares the attributes and/or methods defined in other classes. Inheritance permits the sharing of attributes and methods among similar classes and provides a means of locating a common set of information and behavior in one area. Inheritance is a very important concept of OO technology and is used to distinguish between *object-oriented* languages, those that support inheritance, and *object-based* languages, those that do not support inheritance.

We saw earlier that there are many different pencil objects (wooden, plastic, long, short, etc.) that belong to the class of pencil. However, pencil is not the only thing in our desk drawer that we can use to write—pens and markers are also included. When we look at the various writing instruments, pencils, pens, markers, we see a common set of attributes and behaviors. In this case, all writing instruments have some type of writing tip (felt, lead, ball, etc.), shape (round, square, etc.), length, and weight, and they all can write. So let's create a new class called WritingInstrument that has attributes and methods common to all types of writing instruments (in this case, pencils, pens, and markers). Specifically, all writing instruments have some type of writing tip, are composed of material, have a shape, a length, and a weight, and can write.

Next, we take the Pencil class from Figure 2.1, but we remove the attributes *length, material,* and *shape,* and method **write()** that are inherited from WritingInstrument. The arrow running from Pencil to WritingInstrument is UML notation for the inheritance relationship. In this diagram, Pencil is called a *subclass* or *child* and WritingInstrument is the *superclass* or *parent.* Subclasses (children) inherit from their superclasses (parents). In the UML notation, the arrow points from the subclass to the superclass (see Figure 2.6).

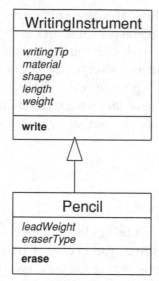

FIGURE 2.6. Subclass and superclass.

NOTES

1. Java permits children to have only **one** parent. This means a subclass can have only one superclass.
2. A child with one parent is called *single inheritance*. If a child has more than one parent, it is called *multiple inheritance*. Java does *NOT* support multiple inheritance.
3. A child can also have children. If a subclass has subclasses, then it is *both* a superclass and a subclass. Its subclasses can inherit attributes and methods from its superclass.

Now, let's add classes to illustrate the importance of inheritance. From the earlier discussion, pens and markers can be added as subclasses of writing instruments, as illustrated in Figure 2.7. To describe a pen, we would know its ink color, ink type, writing tip, material, shape, length, and weight and we would know that it can write. A marker has a tip size, ink color, writing tip, material, shape, length, and weight, and can write. Notice that all three subclasses inherit writing tip, material, shape, length, and weight attributes and the write method from their superclass.

Inheritance is often depicted as a hierarchical structure (as shown in Fig. 2.7), and is referred to as an *IS-A* relationship. The IS-A name is derived from the way in which the diagram is translated in prose: a pencil *IS-A*

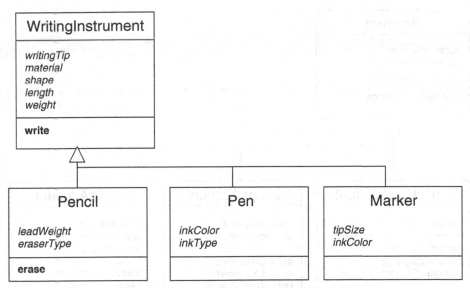

FIGURE 2.7. Subclasses of WritingInstrument.

writing instrument, a pen *IS-A* writing instrument, a marker *IS-A* writing instrument.

In the Community National Bank system we noted earlier that we have three types of accounts: checking, savings, and loan. In addition, these accounts share common attributes and methods. Specifically, referring to Figure 2.5, we see that all three have *accountNumber* and *currentBalance* attributes and the method **getCurrentBalance()**. We can then create a superclass named Account, and place these shared attributes and method there. The new diagram is shown in Figure 2.8.

The interpretation of the diagram would be that a savings account is an account, a checking account is an account, and a loan account is an account. All accounts have an account number and a current balance and can tell you their current balance. These attributes and this method are *inherited* by the three subclasses of Account.

Inheritance is extremely important in OO development for two reasons. First, the maintenance task is greatly simplified. By abstracting common attributes and behaviors, we can localize changes. Using the CNB example, suppose we want to track the date the account was opened. We need only add this attribute to Account and it will be inherited by all subclasses. What if the bank decides to offer two types of loan accounts, say home loans and automobile loans? We simply create these two subclasses under the existing

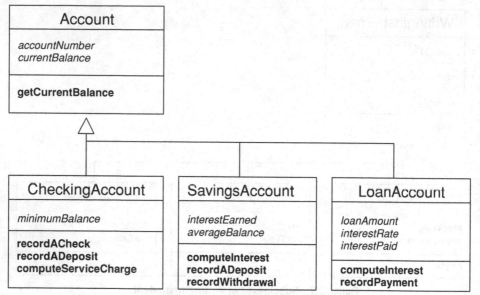

FIGURE 2.8. Subclasses at CNB.

LoanAccount and include only those attributes and methods unique to the new classes.

Second, inheritance gives us an excellent tool for code reuse. We have the attributes and methods written only once. We then reuse them taking advantage of inheritance.

Aggregation

Suppose we had a situation in which it was necessary to show a PC (personal computer) consisting of a keyboard, a monitor, and one or more secondary storage devices. One way would be to create a PC class with each of these items as attributes (as well as the typical attributes of *manufacturer*, *datePurchased*, etc.), as shown in Figure 2.9.

If we need more information beyond one simple fact about a keyboard, such as the model number, then the preceding class structure will not work. The *keyboard* attribute, as part of PC, only allows for a single value. If more information is needed about the keyboard, such as number of keys and manufacturer, then a new class for keyboards should be created. For discussion purposes, let's assume that we need to know various pieces of information about keyboards, monitors, and storage devices. Each of those classes

FIGURE 2.9. The PC class containing all attributes.

could be constructed as shown in Figure 2.10 (for simplicity, no methods are shown).

Now, we want to show these classes as components of the PC class. Using the UML notation, aggregation is shown in Figure 2.11. In this case, the diagram is interpreted as follows: a PC consists of a keyboard, a monitor, and one or more storage devices. Conversely, one can say a keyboard is part of a PC, a monitor is part of a PC, and a storage device is part of a PC. The diamond symbol indicates aggregation and is connected to the class that contains the parts (often called the **WHOLE**, in the *PART-WHOLE* relationship). The PC is the WHOLE; keyboard, monitor, and storage device are the PARTS. The numbers/characters on the lines connecting the parts indicate the number of parts involved in the relationship. An indication of the number of objects of a class involved in a relationship is called *multiplicity*. Multiplicity can be stated as follows:

1	==	only 1
n	==	only *n* number can be involved (*n* can be any number)
*	==	zero or more
1..*	==	1 or more

Keyboard	Monitor	StorageDevice
numberOfKeys manufacturer	resolution manufacturer	type capacity speed

FIGURE 2.10. Classes for PC components.

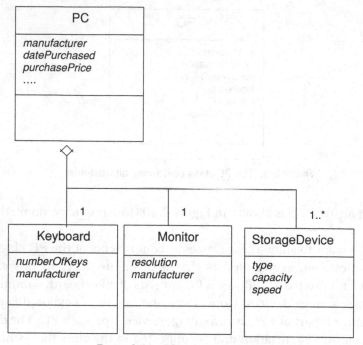

FIGURE 2.11. PC and components.

n..*	==	*n* or more, where *n* is specified
n..m	==	*n* to *m*, where both *n* and *m* are specified

In the example in Figure 2.11, a PC has one (and only 1) keyboard, one (and only 1) monitor, and one or more storage devices.

NOTES

1. An aggregation relationship does not involve inheritance.
2. In the example, a keyboard does not inherit attributes or behaviors from the PC. It is a part of the PC, but it does not share the PC's structure and behavior.

Association

In many cases, classes are related without sharing attributes or behaviors (i.e., inheritance), or without being a part of, or containing, other classes

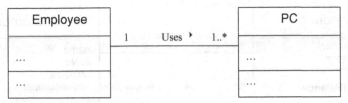

FIGURE 2.12. An association relationship.

(i.e., aggregation). In these cases, the relationship is simply an *association*. An association indicates a connection (not considered inheritance or aggregation) between two or more classes. For example, an employee uses a PC (Figure 2.12).

Multiplicity is interpreted as illustrated previously with aggregation. The diagram in Figure 2.12 is interpreted as follows: an employee uses one or more PCs; a PC is used by only one employee. This relationship involves two classes, and is thus termed a binary association. Note that a class can have an association with itself (i.e., a unary association), two (binary association) classes, three (ternary association) classes, or more than three (*n*-ary association) classes. It is beyond the scope of this book to introduce and explain the various types and details of associations. We encourage you to seek additional sources illustrating UML notation (for example, see the book by Arlow and Neustadt listed in the bibliography at the end of the chapter).

Returning to the CNB example, we need to complete the class diagram by adding the Customer class to the inheritance hierarchy. In this example, a customer *owns* one or more accounts; an account can only be owned by one customer (we realize that, in reality, most accounts can have more than one owner; for simplicity, we are limiting each account to one owner). Figure 2.13 illustrates the complete (at this point) class diagram from the CNB example.

OBJECT COMMUNICATION

Objects communicate by sending messages that invoke methods. In fact, OO systems operate by object communication—without object communication, the system does not function. Thus, it is important to know what objects are capable of doing (their methods) and how to communicate (send messages) with that object. In general, a *message* consists of the object's name, a

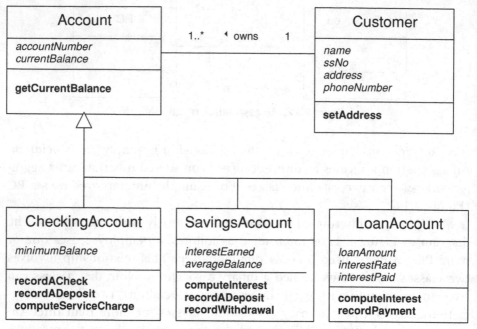

FIGURE 2.13. A more complete CNB class diagram.

method name, and required arguments. For example, to change the customer's address in our CNB example, the following message (in Java syntax) would be used:

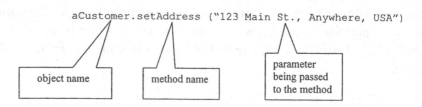

If the <u>Customer</u> class does not contain the method **setAddress()**, then the communication fails, unless it inherits the method from a superclass. In this case, <u>Customer</u> does not inherit any attributes or methods. Notice that we direct the message to an object rather than the class. This is done because the method **setAddress()**, applies to a specific customer, not the general group of customers the class represents.

Suppose that we wish to know the current balance in our checking account, then the message to be used would be:

```
aCheckingAccount.getCurrentBalance()
```

The message is sent to the checking account; but looking at Figure 2.13, we see that <u>CheckingAccount</u> does not have the specified method **getCurrentBalance()** and is unable to satisfy the request. In this case, <u>CheckingAccount</u> will look to its superclass, <u>Account</u>, for help. <u>CheckingAccount</u> inherits the method **getCurrentBalance()** from its superclass, <u>Account</u>.

Notice that the sender of the message, the client, does not know (or care) how the message request is satisfied. For example, when the message is sent to <u>CheckingAccount</u>, the sender is unaware that <u>Account</u> actually satisfies the request. Additionally, the sender does not know how the request is satisfied. In fact, the sender should not care who satisfies the request or how the request is satisfied, only that it is accomplished. The sender need know only the name of the object, the method name, and required arguments.

The goal is to protect the data in an object from everything outside the object—only the object's methods are allowed to access the object's data. The hiding of information from everything outside the object, and providing access only via methods, is called *encapsulation* (sometimes referred to as information hiding). Nothing outside the object should be aware of the object's internal structure or how its methods are implemented. Outside the object, others only need to know the object's name, the method name, and the required parameters. In fact, one can think of this as the object's interface to the outside world.

Consider the impact on maintenance that encapsulation provides. If everything is hidden within an object, then the only place a change needs be made is inside the object—nothing outside the object is affected unless the object interface changes (which, it never should!). For example, using our CNB example, we could add the attribute *dateOpened* to <u>Account</u> without affecting anything outside of the account class. We could also change the manner in which the current balance is stored, but nothing outside the account class would be affected.

POLYMORPHISM

Polymorphism means that the same message can elicit a different response, depending on the receiver of the message. Using the CNB example, both

<u>SavingsAccount</u> and <u>LoanAccount</u> have methods called **computeInterest()**. Thus, we could send the following messages:

```
aSavingsAccount.computeInterest()
aLoanAccount.computeInterest()
```

The method name, **computeInterest()**, is the same, but the receiver of the message is different. Will both messages be handled the same way? One would hope not! The savings account's interest is based on an average monthly balance and varies by current interest rates. A loan's interest is based on a fixed interest rate (CNB does not have variable rate loans). The procedure for calculating interest for a savings account is different from calculating interest for a loan. Thus, the receiver of the message—<u>SavingsAccount</u> or <u>LoanAccount</u>—determines how the message is satisfied. Remember, because of encapsulation, those outside the object do not know how the message is satisfied (the methods could be exactly the same—we would not know!). Polymorphism provides a very consistent and natural way to use messages without worrying about how or who satisfies the message. A message is sent to an object and the object handles it. It is confusing to use specific messages such as **computeSavingsInterest()** and **computeLoanInterest()**, when, in reality, they are both simply **computeInterest()**.

Dynamic Binding

What happens when you compile a COBOL program that has the following statement but in the data division, only X was defined?

```
MOVE X TO Y
```

Of course you get an error, and you can't continue until you define Y. Now, in the context of OO, assume that an object X sends the following message to object Y:

```
Y.doSomething ('data')
```

If, *at compile time*, the compiler (1) finds Y, (2) determines that **doSomething()** is a valid method (either in Y or in its inheritance hierarchy), and (3) links the message to the appropriate memory location (the method), then we have achieved *static binding*. Static binding means that all classes and methods are validated at compile time. Now, consider a different scenario. Y sends the same message, but the compiler does not check the validity. Instead, the message is only *validated at runtime*. In this case, *dynamic binding* is used. Dynamic binding means that the messages are not validated until runtime.

What is the importance of static and dynamic binding? Static binding increases reliability (no runtime crashes due to undeliverable messages) and improves performance (doesn't have to look up the methods), but reduces flexibility (if an object is added or a new message is sent, the program must be recompiled). In contrast, dynamic binding provides increased flexibility, but less reliability and perhaps lower performance. Not all languages support both types of binding. Thus, we must be aware of the language features while developing a system. Java supports both static and dynamic binding. COBOL supports static binding, but has no provision for dynamic association.

SUMMARY OF KEY POINTS IN CHAPTER 2

1. OO is not new but began in the mid-1960s.
2. OOPLs are classified as *pure* or *hybrid*. Pure OOPLs, such as Java and Smalltalk, view everything as an object; hybrids, such as C++ and Object COBOL, are extensions of non-OO languages.
3. In OO development, everything is represented as an *object*. An object contains data (attributes) and a set of operations (methods). An *instance* is a specific object (e.g., aDog is an object of the class <u>Dog</u>). A *class* is a set of objects that share a common structure and a common behavior (e.g., a dog object, aDog, belongs to the class of all dogs). Classes represent an abstraction; it is the essence of the object.
4. *Inheritance* is a relationship among classes where one class shares the attributes and/or behaviors defined in one (single inheritance) or more (multiple inheritance) other classes. Classes are represented via a hierarchy that shows the inheritance from one class to another. An inheritance relationship is also referred to as an *IS-A*, or generalization/specialization relationship.
5. There are three primary forms of relationships among classes: (1) inheritance, (2) aggregation, and (3) association. *Aggregation*, also referred to as HAS-A, CONSISTS-OF, and PART-WHOLE, is used to illustrate a relationship among classes wherein one class is a component of another class. An

association is a relationship between classes that is not an inheritance or aggregation, but rather a general linkage between classes.
6. Objects communicate by sending *messages* that invoke methods. When we send a message, we don't know how or where it will be satisfied.
7. Information hiding is called *encapsulation*. Encapsulation means an object's data is hidden within, and protected by, a shell of procedures.
8. *Polymorphism* means that the same message can elicit different responses depending on the object receiving the message. This allows common names to be used for methods (such as start, stop, run, etc.).
9. *Dynamic binding* means that the messages are not validated until runtime. This allows greater flexibility in adding objects and messages to the system, but it can reduce reliability and performance. *Static binding* means messages are resolved at compile time.

BIBLIOGRAPHY

Arlow, J., and Neustadt, I. (2001). *UML and the Unified Process: Practical Object-Oriented Analysis*. Redwood City, CA: Benjamin/Cummings Publishing.

Booch, G. (1994). *Object-Oriented Analysis and Design with Applications*. Redwood City, CA: Benjamin/Cummings Publishing.

Booch, G. (1986). "Object Oriented Development," *IEEE Transactions on Software Engineering*, SE-12 (2), 211–21.

Deitel, H. M., and Deitel, P. J. (2003). *Java: How to Program*, 5th Ed. Englewood Cliffs, NJ: Prentice-Hall.

Doke, E. R., and Hardgrave, B. C. (1998). *An Introduction to Object COBOL*. New York: John Wiley & Sons.

Kay, A. C. (1993). "The Early History of Smalltalk," *SIGPLAN Notices*, 28(3), 69–95.

CHAPTER 3

Java Structure

OBJECTIVES

In this chapter you will study:

- Java program structure;
- Writing class programs;
- Writing Java comments;
- Naming rules & conventions;
- Calling methods;
- Creating objects; and
- Working with subclasses.

The purpose of this chapter is to introduce you to the structure of Java programs. You will see how to write and execute simple Java programs. By working with real functioning programs, instead of just code segments, you will quickly learn the major structural differences between COBOL and Java.

This chapter begins with a program that models the Customer class from the Community National Bank system introduced in Chapter 2. This program is used to illustrate Java program structure.

We will show you how to write Java comments and review the simple rules for naming variables, methods, classes, and programs. We will also explain the Java coding conventions and style guidelines that will greatly improve the readability of your programs.

We will then execute methods in the customer class program to show how objects are created and to demonstrate calling methods. We will conclude the chapter by developing programs for the account and checking account classes to illustrate working with subclasses.

This chapter assumes you understand the following:

COBOL:
    COBOL program structure
    Column restrictions—area A and B
    Continuation column 7
    Comments and remarks
    Uses of periods, commas, parentheses, spaces
    Scope terminators
    Rules for programmer-supplied names
Java:
    OO concepts (Chapter 2)

A CLASS PROGRAM

Chapter 2 introduced object-oriented concepts and described classes and objects. You also read about the Community National Bank's classes. The class diagram for CNB is presented again here.

Programs that model classes are called *class programs* and are written to define the attributes and methods for the class they represent. For Figure 3.1, for example, we would write five class programs, one for each of the classes shown. A class program consists of Java code that defines attributes (also known as *instance variables*) and operations (also known as *instance methods*). The attributes essentially identify what is important about the class while the operations define how to access and maintain the values of the attributes.

NOTES

1. In COBOL we use the term *data item* or *field* for attribute.
2. Java and many other languages use the term *variable* for attribute.

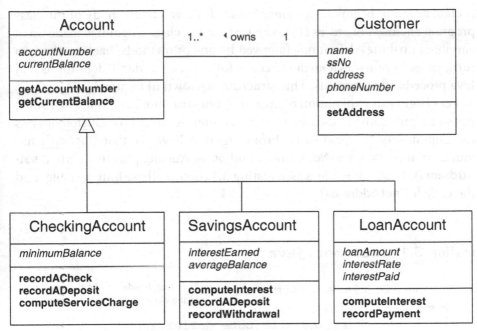

FIGURE 3.1. Community National Bank classes.

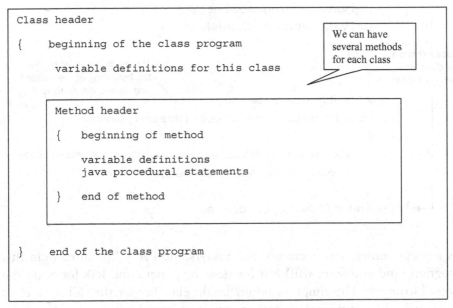

FIGURE 3.2. Java class program structure.

A class program begins with a *class header* followed by the body of the class program enclosed in braces ({}). The body of the class program is made up of variable (attribute) definitions followed by one or methods. Each method, in turn, consists of its own *method header* followed by variable definitions and Java procedural statements. This structure is shown in Figure 3.2.

Let's begin our exploration of Java program structure by looking at a small class program named `Customer.java`, written to model the <u>Customer</u> class for Community National Bank. From Figure 3.1 we see that <u>Customer</u> has four attributes: *name*, *ssNo*, *address*, and *phoneNumber* plus the method **setAddress()**. `Customer.java` (see Listing 3.1) defines these four variables and the code for **setAddress()**.

Listing 3.1: `Customer.java`

```
public class Customer ───── The class header marks the beginning
{                             of the class and names the class
    // customer attribute definitions
    private String name; ───────── Java statements end with ;
    private String ssNo;
    private String address;
    private String phoneNumber;



braces enclose
the class and                          The method header marks
method definitions                     the beginning of the method
                                       and names the method
    // setAddress method
    public void setAddress (String newAdr)
    {
        address = newAddress; ──── Java statements end with ;
    } // end of setAddress method

} // end of Customer class
```

As a programmer, you likely want to understand every line of code in this program (and you soon will) but for now, be patient and let's focus on the overall structure. This simple program has the class header, then all of the class code enclosed in braces. Java makes extensive use of braces to indicate the beginning and end of blocks of code. Within the class definition code we have the attribute definitions and the method code. Notice that braces also surround the method definition code.

As you may suspect, the lines with the double slash (/ /) are comments and we have included them in the program to help you see the various components. In the next section we describe writing comments in more detail.

Notice that the Java statements terminate with a semicolon (;). At first this may seem a bother. However, like the notorious period (.) we use in terminating COBOL statements, the Java semicolon has a very important purpose—it tells the compiler this is the end of the statement. This means that, like COBOL, we can write multi-line Java statements, and simply terminate the statement with the semicolon. This gives us the flexibility of including indentation and white space in our programs to improve readability.

NOTE

Java does not provide us with scope terminating statements such as END-IF, END-COMPUTE, and so forth. We must rely on semicolons and braces to indicate end of statements and blocks of code. Although this may seem at first to be cryptic, you will soon come to appreciate the brevity of this approach.

Let's look at the details of Customer.java beginning with the class header:

This is a *public* class   Its name is Customer

```
public class Customer
```

The class header serves to indicate the start of the class, to name the class, and to define *accessibility* to the class. This header specifies *public* accessibility, which means any other class may access this class.

The four attributes of <u>Customer</u> are defined as:

```
private String name;
private String ssNo;          Don't forget the semicolons!
private String address;
private String phoneNumber;       String is the type of data.
                                  It is similar to COBOL's PIC X
```

As you probably have guessed, the word *private* in each line indicates that no other class or object may *directly* access these attributes—their accessibility is private and strictly controlled. `String` simply means the contents will be alphanumeric (similar to PIC X in COBOL). Following `String` is the name of the attribute, which you will notice matches the attribute names in our class diagram (Figure 3.1). Java calls these statements "variable definition statements."

NOTES

1. Like COBOL, each Java variable definition must include a data type.
2. Chapter 4 describes Java data definition and data types.

The **setAddress()** method consists of a method header followed by a single statement sandwiched between two braces. The method header appears as:

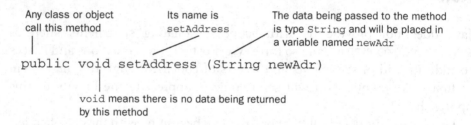

In general, a method header has the following format:

```
access return_data_type method_name (parameter_list)
```

- `access` is either `public` (the method may be called by anyone), `private` (may be called only from within this class), or `protected` (may be called from within this class or its subclasses).
- `return_data_type` indicates the type of data (string, integer, etc.) that will be returned to the method. Only one "piece" of data can be returned, although the data can be a variable, array, or an object. A data type of `void` is also legitimate and indicates that no data are returned.
- `method_name` specifies the name of the method.
- `parameter_list` contains the data types and variable names for the values being passed to the method. The method name combined with the parameter list is called the method signature.

The single statement in **setAddress()** is called an *assignment* statement because it *assigns* or stores a value into a variable. Here, this statement stores the value passed (the new customer address) into the attribute named *address*.

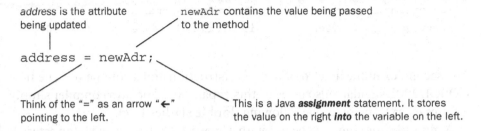

address is the attribute
being updated

newAdr contains the value being passed
to the method

```
address = newAdr;
```

Think of the "=" as an arrow "←"
pointing to the left.

This is a Java *assignment* statement. It stores
the value on the right *into* the variable on the left.

We will demonstrate the execution of this program later in the chapter, but first we want to describe Java structure in a little more detail.

JAVA COLUMN RESTRICTIONS

In general, the column restrictions and margin rules of COBOL are much stricter than Java. For example, COBOL has reserved the first six columns for sequence numbers (page and line numbers carried over from the days of coding forms and punched cards) and the seventh column for comments and continuation characters. COBOL divides the coding line into *Area A* and *Area B*. Certain COBOL code must begin in one area or the other. Fortunately, Java has no such column restrictions.

Like COBOL, good Java programming style suggests that we adopt the practice of using indentation and white space to improve program readability.

WRITING COMMENTS IN JAVA

In order to enhance the program's future maintainability, we will make more use of comments in our Java programs. The Java language provides three types of comments:

1. Single line;
2. Multiple line; and
3. Documentation.

A single line comment begins with two forward slashes (//). Some examples are:

```
// This is a comment line
if (minimumBalance < 500) // The service charge is $5.00
serviceCharge = 5.00F;    // if minimum balance is below $500.00
```

The second example here combines an instruction and a comment. (The new COBOL 2002 standard also gives us this capability.) The Java compiler simply ignores everything on a line following double slashes (//).

A multiple line comment begins with a forward slash followed by an asterisk (/*) and terminates with an asterisk followed be a forward slash (*/). The multiple line comment is a handy tool whenever you want to write several lines of comments in a program. However, it is a little dangerous because when the compiler encounters the slash-asterisk (/*), it assumes everything following is a comment until it detects the terminating asterisk-slash (*/). If you forget to write the */, the compiler will ignore the remainder of your program statements!

```
/*****************************************
*      You can write very long          *
*      comments using the multiple      *
*      line comment                     *
*****************************************/
/*
       You don't need all of the
       asterisks in the previous
       example unless you like
       their appearance
*/
/*     Don't forget to terminate
       multiple line comments or
       the compiler will ignore
       the remainder of your program!
       Oops! The following 'if' is ignored!
       if (minimumBalance < 500)
             serviceCharge = 5.00F;
```

Documentation comments are also multiline, but begin with a slash followed by two asterisks (/**) and terminate with asterisk-slash (*/). These comments are called documentation comments because they can be used to produce program documentation. A supplied program named `javadoc` reads your source program and generates a report containing the documentation comments. This report contains hyperlinks and can be read with a web browser.

NAMING RULES AND CONVENTIONS

Java names for classes, methods, and variables are officially called *identifiers*. Java's rules for naming identifiers are quite simple. An identifier name has only two requirements:

1. It may be as long as you wish but must start with a letter of the alphabet (A–Z, a–z), $, or underscore
2. It may include any character except space (however, we generally avoid using the java operators +, −, *, /).

For example, the following are *not* valid Java identifier names:

- `4Score` (does not begin with a letter, $ or _. Note `fourScore` is OK.)
- `Student Name` (contains a space. `studentName` is OK)

NOTES

1. COBOL programmers are accustomed to using the hyphen (-). Java programmers do not use the hyphen as part of an identifier because the compiler will interpret it as the subtract operator!
2. Be careful—Java is case sensitive. Java makes a distinction between `CustomerName` and `customerName`.

Java programmers, like COBOL programmers, have adopted a *convention* or *style* for writing code. Specific naming conventions have evolved and we suggest you use them in your code. In addition to the obvious rule that all identifiers should be meaningful and descriptive we suggest the following conventions.

- Class names begin with the first word and successive words capitalized:
  `Account`, `SavingsAcount`, `Customer`
- Constant names are all uppercase with an underscore separating each successive word:
  `PRIME_INTEREST_RATE`, `PERCENT_CASH_DISCOUNT`
- Method names begin with lowercase but have the successive words capitalized:
  `tellCurrentBalance`, `computeInterest`
- Variable names begin with lowercase but have the successive words capitalized:
  `customerName`, `currentBalance`, `accountNumber`
- Program names are the class name followed by ".java"(this is actually a *requirement*):
  `Account.java`, `Customer.java`

NOTES

1. Although Java permits us to have more than one class within a program, there can be only one *public* class. The program name is the same as the public class name. In the examples in this book, we use only one class per program.
2. Because both method names and variable names begin with a lowercase letter, we generally include a verb in the method name to indicate its primary task - for example, **recordACheck()** and **computeServiceCharge()**. Note the methods also have parentheses following the name.

CREATING OBJECTS

Chapter 2 made an important distinction between a *class* and an *object*. Recall that a class serves to define the attributes and methods for the class. For example, <u>Customer</u> class represents *all* of the customers of Community National Bank. A <u>Customer</u> object, however, represents a **single specific customer**.

Customer	aCustomer:Customer
name *ssNo* *address* *phoneNumber*	*name* = "Jed Muzzy" *ssNo* = "499444471" *address* = "P.O. Box 1881, Great Falls, MT 59601" phoneNumber = "None"
changeAddress	**changeAddress**

The <u>Customer</u> Class   A <u>Customer</u> Object

FIGURE 3.3. **Customer class and object.**

The class program `Customer.java` describes the four attributes that every customer will have. Each object, however, will have **its own values** for *name, ssNo, address*, and *phoneNumber*.

In order to do any processing for a specific customer, say for Jed Muzzy, we must first create an *object* for Jed. This object will contain values for his *name, ssNo, address*, and *phoneNumber*. Figure 3.3 illustrates both the customer class and an object of the class for customer Jed Muzzy.

We create an object by executing a special method in the class program called a *constructor*. A constructor method is similar to other methods in that it has a method header and statements sandwiched between braces. The constructor method, however, always has the **same name** as the class. The constructor method for <u>Customer</u> is:

The constructor method name is the same as the class name

The parameters passed contain the attribute values for the new object

```
public Customer (String newName, String newSSNo, String
    newAdr, String newPhone)
{
    name = newName;
    ssNo = newSSNo;
    address = newAdr;
    phoneNumber = newPhone;
} // end constructor
```

These assignment statements populate the attributes for this particular customer object

Notice that the constructor method has a slightly different format from other methods. As specified earlier, a method follows the form:

```
access   return_data_type   method_name   (parameter_list)
```

What is missing from the constructor method? The `return_data_type` is not specified. Constructor methods **never** return data. Thus, for constructor headers, a `return_data_type` is not included.

Most Java classes also include methods to report the values of the attributes. Our program, for example, should have methods to tell us the *name, ssNo, address*, and *phoneNumber* of a customer. Methods that report attribute values are called *accessor* methods. Let's add the accessor methods to `Customer.java`.

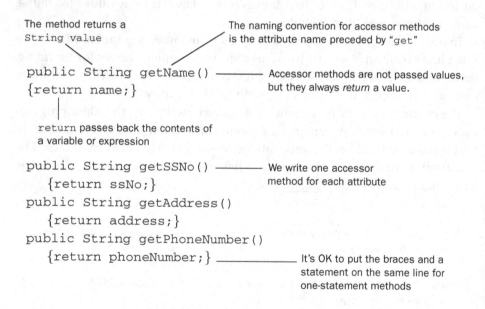

The method returns a
`String value`

The naming convention for accessor methods
is the attribute name preceded by "`get`"

```
public String getName()
{return name;}
```

Accessor methods are not passed values,
but they always *return* a value.

`return` passes back the contents of
a variable or expression

```
public String getSSNo()
   {return ssNo;}
public String getAddress()
   {return address;}
public String getPhoneNumber()
   {return phoneNumber;}
```

We write one accessor
method for each attribute

It's OK to put the braces and a
statement on the same line for
one-statement methods

Java classes also generally include methods to *change* attribute values. These are called *mutator methods*. Their names traditionally begin with "`set`", followed by the variable name. For example, the mutator for *address* is **setAddress()**. Technically, we should also have mutator methods for the other attributes, but have omitted them here for brevity. Feel free to add them yourself.

We now have a complete working class program that models <u>Customer</u> (see Listing 3.2). It has the four attributes, a constructor method to create objects, the mutator method **setAddress()** to change the customer's address, and the four accessor methods to report the attribute values.

Listing 3.2: `Customer.java`

```java
public class Customer
{// customer attribute definitions
  private String name; // private scope limits access
  // to this class
  private String ssNo;
  private String address;
  private String phoneNumber;
  // constructor method to create an object
  public Customer (String newName, String newSSNo,
    String newAdr, String
  newPhone)
  {
    name = newName;
    ssNo = newSSNo;
    address = newAdr;
    phoneNumber = newPhone;
  } // end constructor
  // setAddress mutator method
  public void setAddress (String newAdr)
  {address = newAdr;} // end setAddress
  // accessor methods
  public String getName()
  {return name;}
  public String getSSNo()
  {return ssNo;}
  public String getAddress()
  {return address;}
  public String getPhoneNumber()
  {return phoneNumber;}
} // end Customer.java
```

INVOKING METHODS

As you can see, we write methods to do things—whatever processing is required. A Java method, although different, can be compared to a COBOL subprogram. We execute subprograms in COBOL using the CALL statement and we can pass values to and from a subprogram. Figure 3.4 illustrates the use of a COBOL subprogram to compute an employee's pay.

Similarly, we execute Java methods by calling them and we can pass and receive values. Figure 3.5 shows the execution of a Java method similar to the COBOL example.

In general, we call a method by specifying the name of the object, the method name, and the argument we wish to pass to the method. For example, to change the customer's address in our CNB example, we simply execute the following statement:

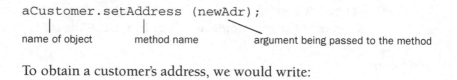

```
aCustomer.setAddress (newAdr);
```
name of object   method name   argument being passed to the method

To obtain a customer's address, we would write:

```
customerAddress = aCustomer.getAddress ();
```

This statement calls the method **getAddress()**, and stores the value returned by the method in the variable *customerAddress*. Of course, the variable *customerAddress* would have to be previously defined.

NOTES

1. An *argument* is the data passed *to* a method.
2. A *parameter* is the data received *by* the method.
3. We pass an *argument* into a *parameter*.
4. The parameter list in the method header creates local variables to contain the argument values being passed to the method. Changing the contents of these variables *does not change* the original argument values.

To illustrate how all of this actually works, let's write a real functioning program to call the various methods in Customer.java. We will name this

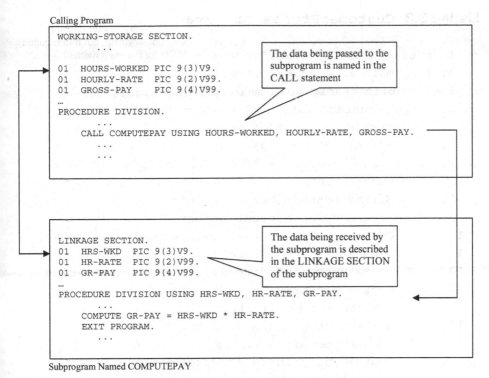

Calling Program

```
WORKING-STORAGE SECTION.
      . . .
01   HOURS-WORKED PIC 9(3)V9.
01   HOURLY-RATE  PIC 9(2)V99.
01   GROSS-PAY    PIC 9(4)V99.
...
PROCEDURE DIVISION.
      . . .
      CALL COMPUTEPAY USING HOURS-WORKED, HOURLY-RATE, GROSS-PAY.
      . . .
      . . .
```

The data being passed to the subprogram is named in the CALL statement

```
LINKAGE SECTION.
01   HRS-WKD  PIC 9(3)V9.
01   HR-RATE  PIC 9(2)V99.
01   GR-PAY   PIC 9(4)V99.
...
PROCEDURE DIVISION USING HRS-WKD, HR-RATE, GR-PAY.
      . . .
      COMPUTE GR-PAY = HRS-WKD * HR-RATE.
      EXIT PROGRAM.
      . . .
```

The data being received by the subprogram is described in the LINKAGE SECTION of the subprogram

Subprogram Named COMPUTEPAY

FIGURE 3.4. Execution of a COBOL subprogram.

new program `CustomerProcessor.java`. This program does not model a class and it has only one method named **main()**. This is a special Java method that is automatically executed when the program is loaded—we don't call it.

```
float hoursWorked;
float hourlyRate;
float grossPay;

grossPay = anEmployee.computePay (hoursWorked, hourlyRate);
```

```
public float computePay (float hrsWkd, float hrRate)
     { return hrsWkd * hrRate; } // compute & return pay
```

FIGURE 3.5. Execution of a Java method.

Listing 3.3: `CustomerProcessor.java`

This parameter doesn't do anything, but it is required for the main method

```
1. public class CustomerProcessor
2. { // main is executed first
3.   public static void main (String args[])
4.   { // customer attribute definitions
5.       String name = "Jed Muzzy";
6.       String ssNo = "499444471";
7.       String address = "P.O. Box 1881, Great Falls,
          MT 59601";
8.       String phoneNumber = "None";
9.       // create an account object
10.      Customer aCustomer = new Customer(name, ssNo,
11.         address, phoneNumber);
12.      // retrieve and display customer information
13.      System.out.println ("Name: " +
          aCustomer.getName());
14.      System.out.println ("SS No: " +
          aCustomer.getSSNo());
15.      System.out.println ("Address: " + aCustomer.
          getAddress());
16.      System.out.println ("Phone: " + aCustomer.
          getPhoneNumber());
17.      // change address then redisplay
18.      aCustomer.setAddress ("P.O. Box 1998, St.
          Louis, MO 63105");
19.      System.out.println ("Address: " + aCustomer.
          getAddress());
20.      } // end main
21. } // end CustomerProcessor.java
```

NOTES

Although the method header for **main()** (line 3) appears a little strange, it is required **as is** by the Java compiler. For now, don't worry about the header.

`CustomerProcessor.java` does five things:

1. Establishes values for the attributes (lines 5–8). These four statements declare the four variables and assign their values.
2. Creates an object of the **Customer** class (line 10). Line 10 calls the constructor method in `Customer.java` and passes it the values for the four attributes. The object reference is then stored in the variable `aCustomer`.

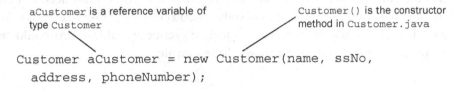

aCustomer is a reference variable of type `Customer`

`Customer()` is the constructor method in `Customer.java`

```
Customer aCustomer = new Customer(name, ssNo,
    address, phoneNumber);
```

An object reference variable, **aCustomer** in this example is simply a variable that contains the memory address of the object. In other words, it is a *pointer* to the memory location of the object. When Java creates an object, memory space is allocated to contain the attribute values for the object.

3. Retrieves and displays attribute values (lines 12–15).

   `println()` is a system method used to display output. Notice we pass the argument (`"Name: "` + `aCustomer.getName()`). Java, working from the inside parentheses out, first executes **getName()** for the object specified by `aCustomer`. Then the literal `"Name: "` is concatenated with the value returned by **getName()**, and this concatenated value is the argument passed to the method `println()`.

4. Changes the address value (line 17).

   Here we simply pass the new address, a literal value this time instead of a variable, to **setAddress()**. The method stores the new address in the attribute *address* for this object.

5. Once more, retrieves and displays the address (line 18).

The output from the program is:

```
Name: Jed Muzzy
SS No: 499444471
Address: P.O. Box 1881, Great Falls, MT 59601
Phone: None
```

NOTE

The CD-ROM included with this book contains a Java compiler plus all of the program examples in the book.

As with all of the programs in the book, we encourage you to not only execute them but also experiment with them by making changes and examining the output. For example, an excellent exercise here is to modify `CustomerProcessor.java` to create **two** objects of the customer class, then execute various methods for **each** object. Note that you do not need to make any changes to `Customer.java`, only to `CustomerProcessor.java`. You will, however need to have two object reference variables. You could use `aCustomer` and `secondCustomer`, for example.

WORKING WITH SUBCLASSES

Recall from Figure 3.1 that the Account class has three subclasses: CheckingAccount, SavingsAccount, and LoanAccount. We show Account and CheckingAccount in Figure 3.6. This class diagram tells us several important things. First, Account is a *superclass* of CheckingAccount and CheckingAccount is a *subclass* of Account. Also, recall from Chapter 2 that the diagram indicates we have an *inheritance* or *IS-A* relationship. A CheckingAccount *IS-A* Account. The subclass CheckingAccount *inherits* methods and relationships from its superclass, Account.

Let's first write a class program for Account. This program will be named `Account.java` and will have two attributes, *accountNumber* and *currentBalance* plus two accessor methods **getAccountNumber()** and **getCurrentBalance()**. In addition, we will add the constructor method named **Account()** and the mutator method **setCurrentBalance()**. We will not include a mutator for *accountNumber*.

Listing 3.4: `Account.java` Program

Abstract means this class will not have an object.
Instead, we create objects of the subclass

```
1. public abstract class Account // abstract classes do
                                  // not have objects
```

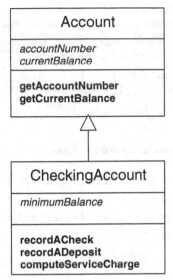

FIGURE 3.6. Account and subclass *CheckingAccount*.

2. {   // account attribute definitions
3. private int accountNumber; // private scope limits
   // access to this class
4. private float currentBalance;

private means only this program has access

5. // constructor method for abstract class only
   // populates attributes

int means data type integer.   float means data type floating point.
Chapter 4 discusses data types.   Chapter 4 discusses data types.

6. public Account (int newAccountNumber, float
   newCurrentBalance)
7. {
8.   accountNumber = newAccountNumber; // populate the
     // attributes
9. currentBalance = newCurrentBalance;
10. } // end constructor
11. // accessor methods

getAccountNumber()   getAccountNumber()
returns as integer value   receives no values

```
12. public int getAccountNumber ()
13. { return accountNumber; }
14. public float getCurrentBalance ()
15. { return currentBalance; }
16. // mutator method
```

protected limits access to this and subclasses

```
17. protected void setCurrentBalance (float
    newCurrentBalance)
18. { currentBalance = newCurrentBalance;} // end
    setCurrentBalance
19. } // end of Account.java
```

Notice that the header for Account.java contains the word abstract. This means that we will not create an <u>Account</u> object. Instead, we create objects from the subclass <u>CheckingAccount</u> that inherits <u>Account</u> methods. Here the superclass exists only so its subclasses <u>CheckingAccount</u>, <u>SavingsAccount</u>, and <u>LoanAccount</u> can inherit from it.

The accessibility for the attributes is private in this program. *Private accessibility* means only this program may access the attribute. Other programs must use the accessor methods to obtain attribute values such as the balance and account number. This example illustrates *data encapsulation*.

Next, let's write the class program for <u>CheckingAccount</u>. This program has only one attribute, *minimumBalance* and five methods. It has a constructor method, an accessor method, **getMinimumBalance()**, plus two *custom methods*, **recordACheck()** and **recordADeposit()**. A custom method is one we write to do some processing, such as record a check or deposit. To keep this example simple and the program a little smaller, we have omitted the custom method **computeServiceCharge()**. We will, however, develop this method later in Chapter 6.

Listing 3.5: CheckingAccount.java

extends Account means CheckingAcccount is a subclass of <u>Account</u>

```
1. public class CheckingAccount extends Account
   // superclass is account
```

```
 2. { // class variable
 3.    private float minimumBalance;
       // private limits access to this class
 4.    // constructor method
 5.    public CheckingAccount (int newAccountNumber,
          float newCurrentBalance)
 6.    { // invoke account constructor to populate
          // account attributes
 7.       super (newAccountNumber, newCurrentBalance);
          // super is the superclass
 8.       minimumBalance = newCurrentBalance;
          // set checkingAccount attribute
 9.    } // end constructor
10.    // accessor method
11.    public float getMinimumBalance ()
12.    { return minimumBalance; }
13.    // post a check to this account
14.    public void recordACheck (float checkAmount)
15.    {
16.       float balance = getCurrentBalance();
          // retrieve balance
17.       balance = balance - checkAmount;
          // subtract check
18.       setCurrentBalance(balance);
          // store new balance
19.    } // end recordACheck
20.    // post a deposit to this account
21.    public void recordADeposit (float depositAmount)
22.    {
23.       float balance = getCurrentBalance();
          // retrieve balance
24.       balance = balance + depositAmount;
          // add deposit
25.       setCurrentBalance(balance);
          // store new balance
26.    } // end recordADeposit
27. } // end of checking account class
```

Let's look a little closer at one of the custom methods, **recordACheck()**.

```
// post a check to this account
public void recordACheck (float checkAmount)
{
   float balance = getCurrentBalance();
   // retrieve balance
   balance = balance - checkAmount; // subtract check
   setCurrentBalance(balance); // store new balance
} // end recordACheck
```

recordACheck() does three things:

1. Retrieves the balance from the account object;
2. Subtracts the check from the balance; and
3. Stores the new balance in the object.

Notice that the method calls **getCurrentBalance()** to retrieve the account balance and store it in the variable `balance`. **getCurrentBalance()** is inherited from <u>Account</u>. The method resides in `Account.java`, not in `CheckingAccount.java`. Similarly, **recordACheck()** calls the inherited method **setCurrentBalance()** to store the new balance.

Finally we write a little program named `AccountProcessor.java` to create a checking account object, then execute methods in `CheckingAccount.java`.

Listing 3.6: `AccountProcessor.java`

```
1. public class AccountProcessor
2. {
3.    public static void main (String args[])
      // main is the first method executed
4.    {
5.       // attribute values
6.       int accountNumber = 12345;
7.       float currentBalance = 50.00F;
```

"F" means the value is floating point

anAccount is a variable containing the memory address of the object

```
8.       // create a checking account object
```

```
9.         CheckingAccount anAccount = new
           CheckingAccount
10.        (accountNumber, currentBalance);
```

pass the account number and balance
to the constructor method

```
11.        // retrieve and display current balance
12.        System.out.println ("Beginning Balance: " +
13.          anAccount.getCurrentBalance());
14.        // post $20 check then retrieve and display
           // current balance
15.        anAccount.recordACheck (20.00F);
```
notice we pass a
literal, but we could
pass a variable

```
16.        System.out.println ("Balance After $20
             check:"+
17.        anAccount.getCurrentBalance());
18.        // post $15 deposit then retrieve and display
           // current balance
19.        anAccount.recordADeposit (15.00F);
20.        System.out.println ("Balance After $15
21.          deposit:" + anAccount.getCurrentBalance());
22.    } // end main
23. } // end accountProcessor.java
```

As you can see, this program does several things:

1. Creates a checking account object with account number 12345 and a current balance of $50.00 (line 9).
2. Retrieves and displays the current balance (line 11).
3. Records a $20 check (line 13).
4. Retrieves and displays the current balance (line 14).
5. Records a $15.00 deposit to the account (line 16).
6. Again retrieves and displays the current balance (line 17).

The output from AccountProcessor.java is:

```
Beginning Balance: 50.0
Balance After $20 check: 30.0
Balance After $15 deposit: 45.0
```

SUMMARY OF KEY POINTS IN CHAPTER 3

1. Java programs that model classes are called *class programs*. Class programs must have the same name as the class they represent, with the .java extension. For example, the class program for Account is Account.java.

2. Class programs consist of a class header followed by the class attribute (variable) definitions and one or more methods. Methods consist of variable definitions and Java procedural code. Java uses braces ({}) to enclose class and method definitions.

3. Java lacks the column restrictions of COBOL. Statements may begin and end in any column. Java statements terminate with a semicolon (;).

4. Java has three different types of comments:
   Single line—begin with double slash
   ```
   // this is a comment
   ```
   Multiple line—begin with slash-asterisk and end with asterisk-slash
   ```
   /* this is a multi-line
   comment */
   ```
   Documentation—begins with a slash-double asterisk and ends with asterisk-slash.
   ```
   /** this is an example of
   a documentation comment */
   ```

5. The names of Java classes, methods, and variables are called *identifiers*. An identifier may be any length but must begin with a letter or & or underscore and may include any character but space.

6. Access to Java classes, methods, and variables is either *public* (all programs have access), *private* (only this class has access), or *protected* (this class and its subclasses have access).

7. There is an important distinction between a *class* and an *object*. A class such as Account represents the attribute definitions and method code for all accounts. An Account object, on the other hand, represents a *specific* customer's account and will contain the *values* for the account number and current balance of the account.

8. We write a special method called a *constructor* to create objects from a class. It has the same name as the class.

9. We write *accessor* methods to report attribute values for specific objects, *mutator* methods to change attribute values, and *custom* methods to do processing.

10. Java methods are executed by calling them, similar to calling COBOL subprograms. The Java call statement has the following format:
    `object_name.method_name (argument_list)`
11. *Arguments* are passed to methods and *parameters* are received by methods.
12. Subclasses *inherit* from their superclass. We define superclasses as *abstract* to indicate that objects of the superclass will not exist.
13. A method name combined with the parameter list is called the *method signature*.
14. The Java *assignment* statement *assigns* or stores a value into a variable.

CHAPTER 4

Defining Data

OBJECTIVES

In this chapter you will study:

- Defining Java data;
- Java data types;
- Variable scope;
- Using literals;
- Defining constants;
- Changing data types; and
- Using Java's **String** class.

In this chapter you will learn how to define data using Java. We will write data definition statements for alphanumeric, numeric, and boolean data (arrays are described and illustrated in Chapter 8). You will also see how to use a supplied Java class named **String** to simplify the definition and manipulation of alphanumeric data. You will also learn about the *scope* of variables. *Scope* determines which parts of your program can access a variable or method.

At the end of the chapter we will develop the complete data definition statements for the attributes of the Community National Bank classes developed in the previous chapter.

NOTES

1. COBOL uses the term *data item* or *field*.
2. Java uses the term *variable*.
3. In keeping with the spirit of Java, here we will use *variable*.

This chapter assumes you know about:

COBOL
    Data division code
    Picture clauses
    Usage clause
    Bits and bytes
Java
    Object-oriented concepts (Chapter 2)
    Java program structure (Chapter 3)

COBOL PICTURE CLAUSE

Those of us who write COBOL programs are accustomed to using the
PICTURE clause to describe data items. The PICTURE clause, always contained in the data division of a COBOL program, establishes the *data type* of
data (numeric or alphanumeric), the size of the data item, and the number of
decimal positions for numeric values and indicates if the item is signed. To
illustrate:

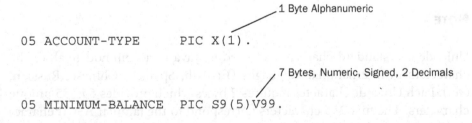

```
                                           1 Byte Alphanumeric

   05 ACCOUNT-TYPE      PIC X(1).

                                           7 Bytes, Numeric, Signed, 2 Decimals

   05 MINIMUM-BALANCE   PIC S9(5)V99.
```

COBOL also uses the terms *group item* and *elementary item*. In the following
example, ACCOUNT-INFORMATION is a group item while ACCOUNT-TYPE and
MINIMUM-BALANCE are elementary items. A group item is simply a concatenation of elementary items.

```
01 ACCOUNT-INFORMATION.
05 ACCOUNT-TYPE          PIC X(1).
05 MINIMUM-BALANCE       PIC S9(5)V99.
```

In addition, COBOL has a USAGE clause to specify how data is stored such as USAGE DISPLAY and USAGE COMP-3.

DEFINING JAVA VARIABLES

Java's data definition is somewhat different from COBOL's. Like COBOL, all variables must be defined as a specific *data type*. However, variables are declared in a different way.

Unlike COBOL, Java has no data division, which means that we can define our variables anywhere in the program. However, good programming style recommends we write data definition code at the beginning of our program.

In Chapter 3 you saw that the rules for writing Java variable names are quite similar to those for writing COBOL: no imbedded spaces, limited use of special characters, first character must be alphabetic. One of the most important things to keep in mind when specifying variable names is to use descriptive names. A variable name of X does not say much about the purpose of a variable; customerName is a much better variable name. Naming rules and conventions for Java identifiers were discussed in detail in Chapter 3.

Java has eight basic (Java uses the term *primitive*) data types grouped into four general categories: two are numeric, one is alphanumeric, and one is Boolean. Table 4.1 lists the details.

NOTE

Unicode is a standard character set used by Java to accommodate all of the characters in international languages (English, Spanish, Chinese, Russian, etc.). Each Unicode character requires 2 bytes which provides 65,535 unique characters. The first 255 characters correspond to the familiar ASCII character set.

We define a Java variable by simply specifying its data type and name using the following format:

```
datatype variablename;
```

TABLE 4.1. Java Data Types			
Category	Type	Range of Values	Size
1. Integer	int	± 2.1 trillion	4 bytes
	short	± 32 thousand	2 bytes
	long	± 9 E18	8 bytes
	byte	± 127	1 byte
2. Floating Point	float	± 3.4 E±38	4 bytes, 7 decimal positions
	double	± 1.79 E±308	8 bytes, 15 decimal positions
3. Character	char	any Unicode*	2 bytes
4. Boolean	boolean	true/false	

To define our account number, for example, we write:

```
int accountNumber;
```

variable data type is integer

variable name is accountNumber

COBOL Equivalent:

```
05 ACCOUNT-NUMBER PIC 9(5).
```

Similar to COBOL, we can also assign a value to a variable when we write its definition.

```
int accountNumber = 12345;
```

COBOL Equivalent:

```
05 ACCOUNT-NUMBER PIC 9(5)
   VALUE 12345.
```

type is floating point

```
float minimumBalance = 50.00F;
```

we use "F" to indicate a floating point value

COBOL Equivalent:

```
05 MINIMUM-BALANCE PIC S9(5)V99
VALUE 50.00.
```

Some other examples of Java data definition are:

```
boolean businessAccount = true;
char billingCycle = 'M';
```

NOTES

1. Single character data values are enclosed in single quotes:
   ```
   char billingCycle = 'M';
   ```
2. The data type `char` is used only for *single* characters. Use the `String` class for multiple characters.
3. Character strings, discussed a little later in this chapter, are enclosed in double quotes (note that `String` must be capitalized since it is the name of a Java class):
   ```
   String customerName = "Jed Muzzy";
   ```

WRITING JAVA LITERALS

Writing literals in Java is very similar to COBOL. For example, when we wanted to store a value of `12345` in the *accountNumber* variable, we simply wrote the value `12345` and assigned it to the variable:

```
int accountNumber = 12345;
```

As we said in Chapter 3, we call this an *assignment statement* because it assigns a value to the variable. We use the `VALUE` clause or a `MOVE` statement to assign values to variables in COBOL.

When we write a literal value, Java makes some assumptions about the data type of the value that we are writing. We can override this assumption by explicitly writing the data type. For example, when we previously wrote

```
float minimumBalance = 50.00F;
```

We included the "F" after the value to specify a data type of `float`. This is because Java *assumes* that literal values with decimals, such as 50.00, are type `double`. Because we wanted to use type `float`, we wrote the "F" after the value to tell Java it was a floating point value.

We did not have to indicate the value was integer in the statement

```
int accountNumber = 12345;
```

Java assumes that numbers without decimals are data type `int` (integer).

THE SCOPE OF VARIABLES

The *scope* of a variable determines its accessibility by other parts of your program.

Scope in Java is more of an issue than in COBOL because we make much greater use of scope with Java. For example, Java variables can have *class scope*, *object scope*, *method scope*, or even *instruction scope*! Where and how we define a variable determines its scope. As we define variables in program examples, we will emphasize their scope for you.

If we declare a variable within a Java statement, its scope is limited to that statement. *Instruction scope* is discussed more thoroughly in subsequent chapters.

Variables declared within a method have *method scope*. They are accessible only to the method where they are declared. This is in sharp contrast to COBOL where a data item declared in the data division can be accessed by the entire program. Incidentally, variables declared within a method *are erased* when the method terminates. In other words, method scope variables exist *only while the method is executing.*

Class scope exists for variables declared within a class program but outside all methods. All methods within the class have access to variables with class scope. Generally, these variables represent *attributes* and each time we create an object, we get another set of variables. In other words, we have a set of variables with their individual values for each object. For example, each object of __Customer__ will have its own values for *name*, *ssNo*, *address* and *phoneNumber*.

If, however, we want to have *only one copy* of a variable for a class, regardless of the number of objects, we specify the variable as *static*. Static variables are also called *class variables* because only one copy of the variable exists for the entire class. To illustrate, assume we have a class variable for the prime interest rate for loan accounts. (We will apply the same prime rate to all accounts.) We declare the variable as:

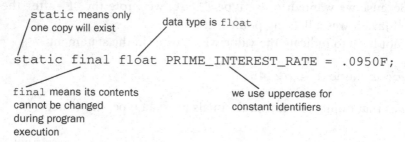

When we use the keyword `static` in defining a variable, or constant, it means the variable applies to the class as a whole and is not associated with an individual object. There is only *one* copy of the variable—individual objects will not have separate copies.

DEFINING JAVA CONSTANTS

Just like COBOL, Java permits us to define variables with a constant data. However, once we define a constant, Java does not permit us to change its value. The general format for defining a Java constant is:

```
final datatype CONSTANT_NAME = value;
```

The keyword `final` means the variable value *cannot* be changed—
this is the *final* value. The Java compiler will not allow statements
that attempt to change it.

For example when we write:

```
final char BILLING_CYCLE = 'M';
```

we define a character variable named `BILLING_CYCLE`, initialize it to a value of "M" and then do not allow its value to be changed. Here we follow the Java style of capitalizing constant names, and we separate the words within the name with the underscore character.

STRING VARIABLES

We previously described the eight *primitive* Java data types and said that a character string of data (an alphanumeric value such as a person's name) uses the String class provided by Java. This class provides us with several nice tools for manipulating strings, as we shall see shortly. Incidentally, String objects are called *complex* data types in Java, meaning that they can contain either simple or other complex data types. For example, a String object consists of one or more characters.

Actually, when we define and initialize a character string it looks like a primitive data type. However, we cannot do much with the string value unless we use the methods in the String class. For example, we cannot compare the contents of two String objects without using the **equals()** method in String.

The format to define a character string is similar to the other data definition statements:

```
String variablename;
```

Note the class name String is
capitalized—it is case sensitive.

For example:

```
String customerName = "Jed Muzzy";
```

The value is enclosed in
double quotes

COBOL Equivalent:

```
05 CUSTOMER-NAME PIC X(9)
VALUE 'Jed Muzzy'.
```

NOTES

1. The statement
   ```
   String customerName = "Jed Muzzy";
   ```
   creates an object of the String class named customerName.
2. This String object is initialized to the value "Jed Muzzy."
3. As with all objects, we cannot directly access attributes (instance variables)—we must use *methods* defined by the class.

The String class provides us with numerous methods to access, compare and manipulate string values. To list just a few (assume s1 and s2 are two String object reference variables):

`s1.charAt(n)` - returns the character in the string at position n in `s1` (relative to zero)

`s1.equals(s2)` - compares values character by character in `s1` and `s2` and returns either `true` or `false`

`s1.equalsIgnoreCase(s2)` - same as **equals()** method, except case is ignored

`s1.length()` - returns the number of characters in `s1`

`s1.substring(n1,n2)` - returns a string of characters in `s1` beginning at position n1 and ending at n2 (relative to zero)

NOTES

1. The code to invoke a method is:
   `objectName.methodName (argumentList);`
2. The parentheses are required, even if there are no arguments.
3. Like all Java identifiers, method names are *case sensitive.* `substring` and `subString` *are not the same.*

Let's take a look at a small Java program that illustrates the creation and manipulation of a couple of <u>String</u> objects. The program named `StringDemo.java` is shown in Listing 4.1. This program has a single method named **main()** whose purpose is to demonstrate the creation of two <u>String</u> objects and then to illustrate the execution of three <u>String</u> methods: **length()**, **charAt()** and **substring()**.

Listing 4.1: `StringDemo.java`

```
1. public class StringDemo ———— the class header names the class
2. {
3.   public static void main (String args[]) —— main() is the
4.   {                                                first method
5.     String s1 = "COBOL Programmers";             executed when
6.     String s2 = "can learn Java";                the program
7.     System.out.println ("The length of s1 is " +  begins
         s1.length());
```
                    println() is a method of the
                    System.out. class that displays
                    output to the screen
```
8.     System.out.println ("The 7th character of s1
         is " + s1.charAt(6));
```

```
9.    System.out.println (s2.substring (10,13) + " is
      FUN!");
10. } // end of main method
11. } // end of StringDemo.java
```

Let's take a brief look at the program before we run it. The program has only one method named **main()**. The **main()** method is where execution begins when the program is loaded.

Lines 5 and 6 create two <u>String</u> objects named s1 and s2 containing the text "COBOL Programmers" (17 characters) and "can learn Java" (14 characters), respectively.

Line 7 does three things. First it invokes the method **length()** for the object s1, then concatenates the value returned with the literal "The length of s1 is", then invokes the method **println()**. System.out is a special Java class that gives us tools for outputting data.

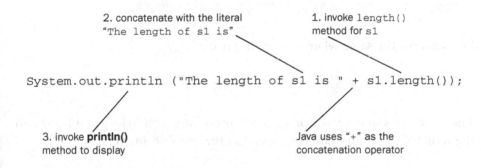

2. concatenate with the literal
"The length of s1 is"

1. invoke length()
method for s1

```
System.out.println ("The length of s1 is " + s1.length());
```

3. invoke **println()**
method to display

Java uses "+" as the
concatenation operator

Similarly, line 8 invokes the **charAt()** method, and line 9 invokes **subString()**. The output from StringDemo.java is:

```
The length of s1 is 17
The 7th character of s1 is P
Java is FUN!
```

NOTES

1. The length of a <u>String</u> object is the number of characters, *not the number of bytes*. Since Java uses Unicode, there are two bytes per character.

2. Remember: the first character is located at position 0 (i.e., everything is relative to 0). Thus, the seventh character of s1 is P, but it is referenced as position number 6.

Similar to <u>String</u>, Java also has a class named <u>StringBuffer</u> that behaves a little more like a COBOL alphanumeric field. You can create a <u>StringBuffer</u> object with a given size and then store data in it, up to the size of the buffer.

CHANGING VARIABLE TYPES

Java gives us the ability to change the data type of a variable. This capability is called *type casting* or simply *casting*. Let's illustrate casting with an example. First, let's take a quick look at using the Java assignment statement to do computation. The COBOL statement

```
COMPUTE ANSWER = 1.5 + INTEGER1 / INTEGER2
```

looks almost the same when written in Java:

```
answer = 1.5 + integer1 / integer2;
```

The same rules of operator precedence apply (division before addition) and the result of the computation is placed in the variable answer.

So, we have a variable named answer we have defined as:

```
double answer;
```

Let's also have two integer variables named integer1 and integer2 defined and initialized as follows:

```
int integer1 = 3;
int integer2 = 2;
```

When we execute the following computation statement, what do you think answer will contain?

```
answer = 1.5 + integer1 / integer2;
System.out.println ("The answer is " + answer);
```

Program output:

```
The answer is 2.5
```

Wait a minute! When we divide 3 by 2 we get 1.5, then when we add 1.5 we get 3—right? Why, then, did we get 2.5 instead of 3? The variables integer1 and integer2 are integer values and the result of the division is 1, not 1.5. Just like in COBOL, the decimal is truncated unless we specify decimal positions.

We can correct this error by *casting* the integer division to type double, which tracks up to 15 decimal positions. Now answer contains 3.

the literal 1.5 is assumed   converts the result of the
to be type double   division to type double

```
answer = 1.5 + (double) integer1 / integer2;
```

Program output:

```
The answer is 3.0
```

The program CastDemo.java executes this example and is shown in Listing 4.2.

Listing 4.2: CastDemo.java

```java
public class CastDemo
{
   public static void main (String args [])
   {
      double answer;
      int integer1 = 3;
      int integer2 = 2;
      answer = 1.5 + integer1 / integer2;
      System.out.println ("The first answer is " +
         answer);
```

```
      answer = 1.5 + (double) integer1 / integer2;
      System.out.println ("The second answer is " +
         answer);
   } // end of main method
} // end of CastDemo.java
```

Program output:

```
The answer is 2.5
The second answer is 3.0
```

In COBOL, if we move a PIC 9(3)V99 field to a PIC 9(1) field, we risk losing data because of truncation. The Java compiler helps us avoid truncation errors when we mix data types in an assignment statement. In general, the compiler permits us to assign a type with a *smaller potential range of values* to a type with a *larger range of values*, but produces an error when we attempt to assign a larger type to a smaller type. To illustrate, two of the four integer data types are byte with a range of −128 to +127 and short with a range of −32,768 to +32,767. We are allowed to assign byte values to short values. For example, given the following variable definitions and value assignments:

```
byte aByteVariable;───────── Range: –128 to +127
short aShortVariable;──────── Range: –32768 to +32767
aByteVariable = 112;
aShortVariable = 128;
```

We can execute the statement:

```
aShortVariable = aByteVariable;─── Value in aShortVariable is 112
```

After executing this statement, aShortVariable is assigned the value of 112.

However, the following statement produces a compiler error because we are at risk of truncation (assuming originally assigned values):

```
aByteVariable = aShortVariable;
```

Valid range = –128 to +127   Value = 128

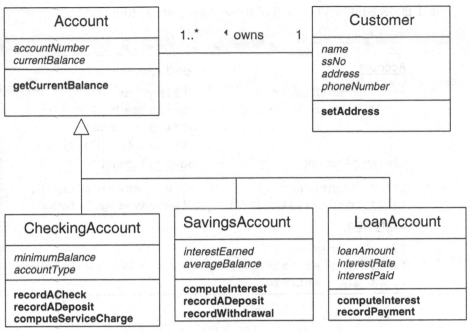

FIGURE 4.1. CNB class diagram.

`aByteVariable` cannot hold a value greater than 127, thus the statement will fail to compile. To rectify this situation, we can override the truncation and perform an explicit type cast with the statement:

```
aByteVariable = (byte) aShortVariable;
```

`aShortVariable` has now been recast as a `byte` type, thus avoiding a truncation problem and a compiler error. However, `aByteVariable` will now hold the value of −128—when the program tries to place the value of 128 in `aByteVariable` (one over the limit of 127), Java rolls it over to the next legal value for a `byte` data type, −128.

VARIABLES FOR COMMUNITY NATIONAL BANK

In Chapter 2 we developed the following class diagram for CNB showing the classes <u>Customer</u>, <u>Account</u>, <u>CheckingAccount</u>, <u>SavingsAccount</u>, and <u>LoanAccount</u>, as illustrated in Figure 4.1.

The data declarations for each of these classes are as follows:

Account	Customer

`int accountNumber;`
`float currentBalance;`
	`String name;`
	`String ssNo;`
	`String address;`
	`String phoneNumber;`

CheckingAccount	SavingsAccount
`int accountType;` `float minimumBalance;`	`float interestEarned;` `float averageBalance;`
LoanAccount	

`float loanAmount;`
`float interestRate;`
`float interestPaid;`	

SUMMARY OF KEY POINTS IN CHAPTER 4

1. Java has eight *primitive* data types grouped into four general categories.

Category	Type	Range of Values	Size
1. Integer	int	± 2.1 trillion	4 bytes
	short	± 32 thousand	2 bytes
	long	± 9 E18	8 bytes
	byte	± 127	1 byte
2. Floating Point	float	± 3.4 E±38	4 bytes, 7 decimal positions
	double	± 1.79 E±308	8 bytes, 15 decimal positions
3. Character	char	any Unicode	2 bytes
4. Boolean	boolean	true/false	

2. We define a Java variable by specifying its data type and name:
`datatype variablename;`
and can assign a value as part of the definition:
`datatype variablename = initialvalue;`

3. The *scope* of a variable determines its accessibility by various parts of a program. Java variables may have *class scope*, *object scope*, *method scope*, and even *instruction scope*. A variable's scope is determined by where it is defined.
4. Use the keyword `static` to declare a class variable. Only one copy of the variable will exist and all methods in the class have access. If you want to have a copy of a variable for each object, omit `static`.
   ```
   static datatype variablename = value;
   ```
5. Use the keyword `final` to define constant data:
   ```
   final datatype CONSTANT_NAME = value;
   ```
6. Character string data are stored in an object of the <u>String</u> class that provides methods to access the data:
   ```
   String variablename = "string value";
   ```
7. The Java compiler will not permit us to use an assignment statement in which truncation may occur without explicitly *casting* the value that may be truncated.

CHAPTER 5

Computation

OBJECTIVES

In this chapter you will study:

- Exceptions;
- Data types;
- Type casting;
- Wrapper classes;
- Arithmetic operators;
- The Math class; and
- The NumberFormat class.

The purpose of this chapter is to introduce you to Java computation. The basic arithmetic operators add, subtract, multiply, and divide (+, -, *, /) are the same as those we use in COBOL's COMPUTE statement. However, Java operations such as exponentiation (raising a value to a power) and rounding are accomplished using methods in the Math class. Java also has operators that enable us to write computation shortcuts if we wish.

Also, you will recall from Chapter 4 that Java is very particular about data types. This sensitivity is raised to a higher level when we do computation, as discussed more thoroughly in this chapter.

The chapter begins with a discussion of Java *exceptions*. An exception is Java's way of informing us of some condition that occurs while our program is running. While doing computation, for example, this could be an error like dividing by zero. Exceptions are not limited to arithmetic, however. You will see how exceptions are used to signal us about any condition, ranging from computation errors to hardware problems. In this chapter we will illustrate the use of custom exceptions using the familiar CheckingAccount class developed in Chapter 3.

Next, we will review Java's primitive data types. Then we will describe and illustrate *wrapper* classes for the primitive data types. Methods in these classes for converting data from numeric to string and back will be explored and demonstrated. We willl then present and discuss the language's arithmetic operators. Changing data types (casting) will also be reviewed and illustrated.

The Math class will be introduced and some of its methods demonstrated. We will also demonstrate how to format numerical data using the NumberFormat class, although this is not directly related to computation. This class has some useful methods for formatting data with commas and dollar signs. We will write a small program to illustrate the use of these methods.

This chapter assumes you understand the following:

COBOL:
    COMPUTE verb
    SIZE ERROR clause
    COBOL edit characters
    Arithmetic operators
Java:
    OO concepts (Chapter 2)
    Java program structure (Chapter 3)
    Defining data (Chapter 4)

EXCEPTIONS

Java uses *exceptions* as a tool to help us deal with errors and conditions that occur while our program is running. Exceptions can be genuine errors

TABLE 5.1. Partial Exception Class Hierarchy

Exception
    IOException (described and illustrated in Chapter 9)
        EOFException
        FileNotFoundException
    RuntimeException
        ArithmeticException (illustrated in Chapter 5)
        NumberFormatException (illustrated in Chapter 5)

such as divide by zero or file not found, or simply situations that we need to do something about, such as end of file or non-numeric data entered by a user.

Like nearly everything else in Java, an exception is an object (of the Exception class, or one of its subclasses) that is created while our program is running. The steps involved with handling exceptions are:

1. Our program executes code that can cause an exception.
2. Java detects the condition, creates an exception object describing the condition, and sends the exception object to our program.
3. Our program recognizes the exception and takes appropriate action. Note that if an exception is produced and sent to our program, and we fail to recognize it, Java will terminate our program.

An exception is an object of a class derived from the Exception class. Part of the class hierarchy appears in Table 5.1. The classes in **boldface** are demonstrated in this chapter (unless otherwise noted).

The process of creating an exception object and sending it to our program is called *throwing an exception*. Our program then *catches the exception* when it receives the exception object and takes appropriate action.

In keeping with this terminology, Java uses a structure called **try-catch** whenever we execute code that has the potential for creating an exception. Incidentally, when we call any method that can throw an exception, we must use the try-catch structure, otherwise the Java compiler generates an error message and will not compile our program. In other words, we must learn to recognize when a method may throw us an exception. The Java API documentation specifies which methods can throw exceptions.

The try-catch structure is shown in Listing 5.1.

Listing 5.1: `try-catch` Structure

```
try
{
   // code that can cause an exception
   // execution transfers to the appropriate catch
   // block when the exception is thrown
}
catch (exception_class reference_variable_name)
{
   // this code is executed only if the specified
   // exception is thrown
}
finally // the finally block is optional
{
   // this code is executed whether or not an exception
   // is thrown
}
```

The code in a catch block will be executed *only if* the specific exception identified in the catch parameter is thrown. For example, if we write a catch block for ArithmeticException it will catch only an ArithmeticException object. It will ignore for example, a NumberFormatException. However, if we catch a superclass of ArithmeticException, say Exception, then it will be caught if an ArithmeticException occurs. Notice that we can have multiple catch blocks—one for each different type of exception we wish to catch. Also, note that whenever a statement in the try block triggers an exception, any remaining statements in the try block *are not executed* and execution goes to the appropriate catch block. In other words, the execution of the try block stops as soon as an exception is thrown.

The following program, named ArithmeticExceptionDemo.java, is a simple example of exception handling for a divide by zero error. The program attempts to divide by zero. However, because we are using the try-catch structure, Java detects the error and transfers control to the catch block. The specific exception being caught is ArithmeticException (refer to Table 5.1). When the error occurs, the catch block is executed and the output is displayed as shown in Listing 5.2. The error description contained in the exception object is "/ by zero."

Listing 5.2: `ArithmeticExceptionDemo.java`

```
public class ArithmeticExceptionDemo
{
    public static void main(String args[])
    {
        int a = 5;
        int b = 0;
        int c = 0;

        try                    division by zero triggers
        {                      the creation of an exception
            c = a / b;
            System.out.println ("Successful divide by
                zero");
        } // end try                the ArithmeticException is caught
        catch (ArithmeticException anException)
        {
            System.out.println ("Caught ArithmeticException"
                + anException);
        } // end catch       anException contains "/ by zero"
    } // end main
} // end ArithmeticExceptionDemo.java
```

The output is:

```
Caught ArithmeticException java.lang.
    ArithmeticException: / by zero
```

If we were to remove the `try-catch` and rerun the program, Java would terminate our program with the message:

```
java.lang.ArithmeticException: / by zero
```

The difference is that if we use `try-catch` to intercept the exception, we can deal with the condition without allowing Java to terminate our program.

Similarly, COBOL uses the ON SIZE ERROR clause to trap computational errors. Rewriting the previous Java code segment in COBOL produces:

```
01 A PIC 9(2) VALUE 5.
01 B PIC 9(2) VALUE 0.
01 C PIC 9(2) VALUE 0.
COMPUTE C = A / B
   ON SIZE ERROR
      DISPLAY "CANNOT DIVIDE BY ZERO"
   NOT ON SIZE ERROR
      DISPLAY "SUCCESSFUL DIVIDE BY ZERO"
END-COMPUTE
```

The output is:

```
CANNOT DIVIDE BY ZERO
```

CUSTOM EXCEPTION CLASSES

There are times when we may wish to use an exception that is not part of the Java exception class hierarchy to deal with some condition we encounter. It is a simple matter for us to define a new exception class and use it in a program.

Recall that the CheckingAccount class for Community National Bank has a method named **recordACheck()** shown again as follows:

```
// post a check to this account
public void recordACheck (float checkAmount)
{
   float balance = getCurrentBalance();
   // retrieve balance
   balance = balance - checkAmount; // subtract check
   setCurrentBalance(balance); // store new balance
} // end recordACheck
```

The logic in this method records a check without considering if the account has a sufficient balance to pay the check. To call this method, we write:

the CheckingAccount object　　amount to be posted

```
anAccount.recordACheck(checkAmount);
```

Let's assume we wish to have **recordACheck()** throw an exception to notify the calling program that the account does not have sufficient funds to pay the check.

We will have **recordACheck()** create and throw a *custom* exception. The steps are:

1. Write a class program for the new custom exception by extending the Exception class. This is a very short program because the only method it needs is a constructor.

NSFException is a subclass of Exception

```
public class NSFException extends Exception
// not sufficient funds
{
    public NSFException (String errorMessage)
    // constructor
    {super(errorMessage);} // call superclass constructor
} // end NSFException
```

2. Add "throws NSFException" to the **recordACheck()** method header. This forces any call to this method to use try-catch.

```
public void recordACheck (float checkAmount) throws
    NSFException
```

3. When insufficient funds are detected, create and throw the exception:

```
if (balance >= checkAmount)
// see if sufficient balance
{ // if yes, record the check
    balance = balance - checkAmount;
    setCurrentBalance(balance); // store new balance
{
else
{ // not sufficient funds — create & throw NSFException
    // NSFException e = new NSFException("Not Sufficient
    // Funds");
```

this message is stored in
the Exception object

```
throw e;
} end if
```
— throw sends the Exception object to the calling program

4. Then when we call **recordACheck()** we must use the `try-catch` structure to detect the insufficient funds exception if it is thrown:

```
try
{
   anAccount.recordACheck(checkAmount);
   // post the check
}
catch (NSFException e)
// catch insufficient funds exception
{
   // do whatever needed for insufficient funds
} // end try-catch
```

`CheckingAccount.java` with the custom exception NSFException added is shown in Listing 5.3. Notice we have changed only the **recordACheck()** method. No other changes are necessary.

Listing 5.3: `CheckingAccount.java` with NSFException

```
public class CheckingAccount extends Account
// superclass is account
{ // attribute definition
   private float minimumBalance;
   // constructor method
   public CheckingAccount (int newAccountNumber,
      float newCurrentBalance)
   { // invoke account constructor to populate account
     // attributes
      super (newAccountNumber, newCurrentBalance);
      minimumBalance = newCurrentBalance;
      // populate attribute
   } // end constructor
   // accessor method
```

```
public float getMinimumBalance ()
{
  return minimumBalance;
}
// method to post a check to this account
public void recordACheck (float checkAmount) throws
  NSFException
{
  float balance = getCurrentBalance();
  if (balance >= checkAmount)
  // see if sufficient funds
  {
    balance = currentBalance - checkAmount;
    setCurrentBalance(balance); // store new balance
  }
  else
  {// if not, throw an exception
    NSFException e =
      new NSFException("Not Sufficient Funds");
    throw e;
  } // end if
} // end method recordACheck

// post a deposit to this account
public void recordADeposit (float depositAmount)
{
  float balance = getCurrentBalance();
  // retrieve balance
  balance = balance + depositAmount; // add deposit
  setCurrentBalance(balance); // store new balance
} // end recordADeposit
} // end of checking account class
```

We then modify AccountProcessor.java from Chapter 3 to utilize the revised **recordACheck()** method. Here we use the try-catch structure to call **recordACheck()**. As you can see, we create a checking account object with an initial balance of $50. Next we post a $20 check and a $15 deposit, leaving a balance of $45. Then we attempt to post a $100 check, but because

the balance is less than the amount of the check, **recordACheck()** throws the
NSFException and the catch block displays the message "Not Sufficient
Funds."

Listing 5.4: `AccountProcessor.java` with `try-catch`

```
public class AccountProcessor
{
   public static void main (String args[])
   // main is executed first
   {
      // attribute values
      int accountNumber = 12345;
      float currentBalance = 50.00F;

      // create a checking account object
      CheckingAccount anAccount = new
         CheckingAccount(accountNumber, currentBalance);
      // retrieve and display current balance
      System.out.println ("Beginning Balance: " +
         anAccount.getCurrentBalance());
      try
      {
         // post a $20 check, retrieve and display
         // balance anAccount.recordACheck (20.00F);
         System.out.println ("Balance After $20 check: "
            + anAccount.getCurrentBalance());
         // post a $15 deposit, retrieve and display
         // balance
         anAccount.recordADeposit (15.00F);
         System.out.println ("Balance After $15 deposit: "
            + anAccount.getCurrentBalance());
         // now try posting a $100 check
         anAccount.recordACheck (100.00F);
         System.out.println ("Balance After $100 check: "
            + anAccount.getCurrentBalance());
      } // end try block
```

TABLE 5.2. Java Numeric Data Types		
Type	Range of Values*	Size
int	±2.1 trillion	4 bytes
short	±32 thousand	2 bytes
long	±9 E18	8 bytes
byte	±127	1 byte
float	±3.4 E±38	4 bytes, 7 decimal positions
double	±1.79 E±308	8 bytes, 15 decimal positions

* Actually, to be precise, the most negative value is 1 more than the value shown here. For example, byte has a range from −128 to +127.

```
        catch (NSFException e)
        {
            System.out.println ("Caught NSFException" + e);
        } // end catch
    } // end main
} // end of accountProcessor.java
```

The output from `AccountProcessor.java` is shown below.

```
Beginning Balance: 50.0
Balance After $20 check: 30.0
Balance After $15 deposit: 45.0
Caught NSFExceptionNSFException: Not Sufficient Funds
```

A REVIEW OF PRIMITIVE DATA TYPES

Chapter 4 described how to define Java data. You will recall that Java has eight primitive data types. Six of these types are numeric, one is alphanumeric, and one is Boolean. In this chapter we focus on the six numeric types. Four of these contain whole numbers (`int, short, long, byte`) and two allow decimal positions (`float` and `double`). Table 5.2 lists the detailed characteristics of these numeric data types.

Also recall from Chapter 4 that Java is very particular about converting one data type to another because it does not want to truncate numerical data without our specific approval and knowledge. The Java compiler helps us

TABLE 5.3. Data Type Value Ranges	
Type	Range
byte	±127
short	±32 thousand
int	±2.1 trillion
long	±9 E18
float	±3.4 E+38
double	±1.79 E+308

avoid truncation errors when we mix data types. In general, the compiler permits us to assign a type with a *smaller potential range of values* to a type with a *larger range of values*, but generates an error when we attempt to assign a larger type to a smaller type. We use *type casting* to convert numeric data from one type to another whenever truncation could occur.

Table 5.3 lists the data types in ascending range of value order. Conversions can be made without explicit casts when going from a lower to a higher type, but not the reverse. Explicit casts are required when converting from a larger range of values to a smaller one. Also, when an arithmetic expression contains mixed data types, Java converts the result to the type with the largest range of values. For example, if we use int and float in an expression, the result must be float.

We can explicitly cast one data type to another. For example, if we have a data type double that we want to convert to float, we could write:

```
aFloatValue = (float) aDoubleValue;
                      Cast to float
```

The contents of aFloatValue will now be type float.

WRAPPER CLASSES

The java.lang class library contains classes for each of the primitive data types. All of these, except Integer, are named the same as their corresponding primitive (int is Integer), with the first letter of the name is capitalized. For example, type double has the class <u>Double</u>, float has <u>Float</u>, etc. Be careful however, because the only difference between the primitive float and the class <u>Float</u>, is the uppercase F!

These classes are often called *wrapper* classes because they *wrap* an object around the data: the data are encapsulated. The object contains a value of the type indicated. For example, an object of the <u>Integer</u> class contains an int value.

The code to create an object of one of these classes looks like that for any other object creation. To create objects of <u>Double</u>, <u>Float</u>, <u>Integer</u>, and <u>Long</u> we write:

```
Double aDouble = new Double(123.456);
Float aFloat = new Float(123.456F);
// we specify "F" for float
Integer anInteger = new Integer (123);
Long aLong = new Long(123456L);
```

It is important to realize however, that these variables (aDouble, aFloat, anInteger, and aLong) are now *object reference variables*. They contain references to objects instead of data values. This means we cannot treat them as data items in computation statements. For example, we cannot write a statement like this:

```
i = anInteger + 1;
```

This is because anInteger does not contain the integer value 123. Instead, it contains a *reference* to an object of the <u>Integer</u> class that contains the integer value 123. If we wish to add 1 to the value contained in the anInteger object and store it in an integer variable i, we must use a *method* to obtain the value stored in the object:

```
i = anInteger.intValue() + 1;
```

anInteger **refers** to or points to the object that contains the integer value 123

intValue() returns the integer value (123) contained in the object

These classes also provide some useful methods to convert numeric data to <u>String</u>. (Remember that a <u>String</u> variable is also a reference variable pointing to an object of the <u>String</u> class.) For example to convert the integer value in anInteger to <u>String</u>, we use the <u>Integer</u> class method **toString()**:

```
String aStringFromInteger;
// declare a String reference variable

aStringFromInteger = new
  \  String(Integer.toString(anInteger.intValue()));
```

we now have a new <u>String</u> object named aStringFromInteger that contains 123

toString() is an <u>Integer</u> class method that converts an integer to a <u>String</u>

intValue() is a method that returns the value in anInteger

We can then convert the string value back to an integer value using the <u>Integer</u> class method **valueOf()**. The following code converts the contents of aStringFromInteger back to int and puts it into a new <u>Integer</u> object named anIntegerFromString:

the <u>Integer</u> object now contains 123

valueOf() converts <u>String</u> to <u>Integer</u>

```
Integer anIntegerFromString = Integer.valueOf
    (aStringFromInteger);
```

Many of these methods will throw an exception if the argument passed is inappropriate. For example, if we try to convert a nonnumeric value with the **valueOf()** method, it will throw a <u>NumberFormatException</u>. In fact, this is a useful technique for detecting nonnumeric data. Try to convert it to <u>Integer</u> using the **valueOf()** method. If it is not numeric, you will catch <u>NumberFormatException</u>. An example of this code is:

```
try
{Integer anIntegerFromString =
   Integer.valueOf(aStringFromInteger);}
catch (NumberFormatException e)
{// do processing for nonnumeric data}
```

Listing 5.5 (`WrapperDemo.java`) demonstrates some of these methods for the wrapper classes.

Listing 5.5: `WrapperDemo.java`

```java
// Demo Data Type Class Methods
// WrapperDemo.java

public class WrapperDemo
{
   public static void main(String args[])
   {
   // create & display objects of Double, Float,
   // Integer, and Long
   Double aDouble = new Double(123.456);
   Float aFloat = new Float(123.456F);
   Integer anInteger = new Integer (123);
   Long aLong = new Long(123456);
   System.out.println("aDouble =" + aDouble);
   System.out.println("aFloat =" + aFloat);
   System.out.println("anInteger =" + anInteger);
   System.out.println("aLong =" + aLong);
   // convert numeric to String & display
   String aStringFromDouble = new
   String(Double.toString(aDouble.doubleValue()));
   String aStringFromFloat = new
   String(Float.toString(aFloat.floatValue()));
   String aStringFromInteger = new
   String(Integer.toString(anInteger.intValue()));
   String aStringFromLong = new
      String(Long.toString(aLong.longValue()));
   System.out.println("aStringFromDouble =" +
     aStringFromDouble);
   System.out.println("aStringFromFloat =" +
     aStringFromFloat);
   System.out.println("aStringFromInteger =" +
     aStringFromInteger);
   System.out.println("aStringFromLong =" +
     aStringFromLong);
   // convert String to numeric & display
   Double aDoubleFromString = Double.valueOf
     (aStringFromDouble);
```

```
  Float aFloatFromString = Float.valueOf
    (aStringFromFloat);
  Integer anIntegerFromString = Integer.valueOf
    (aStringFromInteger);
  Long aLongFromString = Long.valueOf
    (aStringFromLong);
  System.out.println("aDoubleFromString =" +
    aDoubleFromString);
  System.out.println("aFloatFromString =" +
    aFloatFromString);
  System.out.println("anIntegerFromString =" +
    anIntegerFromString);
  System.out.println("aLongFromString =" +
    aLongFromString);
  // do arithmetic with objects
  double d = aDouble.doubleValue() +
    aDoubleFromString.doubleValue();
  System.out.println("d =" + d);
  float f = aFloat.floatValue() + aFloatFromString.
    floatValue();
  System.out.println("f =" + f);
  int i = anInteger.intValue() + anIntegerFromString.
    intValue();
  System.out.println("i =" + i);
  long l = aLong.longValue() + aLongFromString.
    longValue();
  System.out.println("l =" + l);
  } // end main
} // end WrapperDemo.java
```

The output from the program is:

```
aDouble =123.456
aFloat =123.456
anInteger =123
aLong =123456
aStringFromDouble =123.456
aStringFromFloat =123.456
aStringFromInteger =123
```

```
aStringFromLong =123456
aDoubleFromString =123.456
aFloatFromString =123.456
anIntegerFromString =123
aLongFromString =123456
d =246.912
f =246.912
i =246
l =246912
```

ARITHMETIC OPERATORS

COBOL has the COMPUTE statement to do computation, plus individual statements to ADD, SUBTRACT, MULTIPLY, and DIVIDE. Java does computation
using the *assignment statement*, which evaluates an *expression* on the right
side of the assignment operator (=) and stores the result in the variable on the
left side. An expression is simply some combination of operators, variables,
and values that evaluate to a result. Note that unlike COBOL, Java expressions
may evaluate to a boolean value (true or false).

```
result = (expression);
```
                    The expression is evaluated and the
                    result stored in the variable on the left
                    side of the "=" sign.

Java uses the basic arithmetic operators add, subtract, multiply, and divide (+, -, *, /) which are the same as those used in COBOL's COMPUTE
statement. Some examples are:

```
balance = balance - checkAmount;
interestCharged = loanBalance * interestRate;
```

COBOL Equivalent:

```
COMPUTE BALANCE = BALANCE - CHECK-AMOUNT
COMPUTE INTEREST-CHARGED = LOAN-BALANCE * INTEREST-RATE
```

Java provides us with several additional arithmetic operators, as indicated in
Table 5.4.

TABLE 5.4. Java Arithmetic Operators		
Operator	Function	COBOL Equivalent
+	Add	+
−	Subtract	−
*	Multiply	*
/	Divide	/
%	Modulus	Mod function
i++	Post-increment	No direct equivalent
i--	Post-decrement	No direct equivalent
++i	Pre-increment	No direct equivalent
--i	Pre-decrement	No direct equivalent

The modulus operator returns the integer remainder of a division operation. For example the expression 2%1 (i.e., 2/1 = 2, remainder 0) returns 0, but 3%2 (i.e., 3/2 = 1, remainder 1) returns 1.

The *increment/decrement* operators (i++, i--, ++i, --i) are inherited from the C++ language and have no direct COBOL equivalent, although we can do the same things with a little more code. These operators are merely coding shortcuts, but we will explain them here because many Java programmers use them.

The Java language also has *assignment operators*, which are simply the arithmetic operators (+,-, *, /, %) combined with the assignment operator (=). Again, we can do the same thing in COBOL but it requires a little more code. Table 5.5 illustrates these coding shortcuts.

As COBOL programmers, we generally shy away from coding shortcuts that reduce the clarity, and therefore the maintainability, of programs. However, as you become accustomed to these new techniques they become more familiar and seem less cryptic.

THE MATH CLASS

The Math class, a member of the java.lang package, provides several important computational methods. Some of the more popular methods are listed in Table 5.6. Note that those with an asterisk (*) have a corresponding COBOL function (ANSI-85). All of the methods are static (class) methods, which means we do not create an object of the Math class and we call the

	TABLE 5.5. Using Java Shortcut Code	
Java Code	Java Shortcut Code	COBOL Equivalent
i = i + 1;	i++;	COMPUTE I = I + 1
i = i - 1;	i--;	COMPUTE I = I - 1
i = j + 1;	i = ++j;	COMPUTE I = J + 1
i = j;		MOVE J TO I
i = j - 1;	i = --j;	COMPUTE I = J - 1
i = j;		MOVE J TO I
i = i + 2;	i += 2;	COMPUTE I = I + 2
i = i - 2;	i -= 2;	COMPUTE I = I - 2
i = i / 2;	i /= 2;	COMPUTE I = I / 2
i = i * 2;	i *= 2;	COMPUTE I = I * 2
i = i % 2;	i %= 2;	I = MOD(I, 2)

methods using the class name: **Math.random()**, for example. Note that the **round()** method returns a whole number, round(double) returns type long, and round(float) returns type int. This is significantly different than the way the COBOL ROUNDED clause works. COBOL rounds to the number of decimals contained in the result field picture clause.

The Math class also includes methods to do trigonometric and logarithm calculations if you are interested. In addition, it has two static constants:

Math.E contains the base of natural log e
Math.PI contains pi.

	TABLE 5.6. Selected Math Class Methods
Code	Function
abs(x)	Returns the absolute value of an argument
max(x,y)*	Returns the greater of two values
min(x,y)*	Returns the smaller of two values
pow(x,y)	Returns the value of the first argument raised to the power of the second
random()*	Returns a random number between 0 and 1
round(x)	Returns the closest integer value to the argument
sqrt(x)*	Returns the square root of a double value
floor(x)	Returns truncated double value

We illustrate computation and the use of the Math class by writing code to compute the amount of a loan payment for the Community National Bank. If we know the original loan amount (BALANCE), the annual percentage interest rate (APR), and the loan duration expressed in number of months (MONTHS), we can calculate the monthly loan payment (PAYMENT) using the COBOL formula:

APR/12 is the monthly rate

```
COMPUTE PAYMENT =
   (BALANCE * (APR / 12)) / (1 - 1 / (1 + APR / 12) **
      MONTHS
```

In Java we will use the Math class and write: Math.pow(x, y) returns
                                                       x raised to the y power

```
payment = (balance * (apr / 12))/(1 - 1/ Math.pow((1 +
   apr / 12), months));
```

Given the following data,

```
float balance = 1000F;
float apr = .08F;
int months = 6;
double payment = 0;
```

COBOL Equivalent:

```
01 BALANCE PIC 9(5)V99 VALUE 1000.
01 APR PIC V99 VALUE .08.
01 MONTHS PIC 9(2) VALUE 6.
01 PAYMENT PIC 9(5)V99 VALUE ZEROS.
```

The output from the Java computation is:

```
170.57724306813628
```

The output from the COBOL computation is:

```
00170.57
```

If we wanted this value rounded to 170.58 in COBOL, of course, we simply use the ROUNDED option:

```
COMPUTE PAYMENT ROUNDED =
    (BALANCE * (APR/12)) / (1 - 1 / (1 + APR / 12) **
      MONTHS.
```

The output from this COBOL computation is now:

```
00170.58
```

We can round the payment to 170.58 in Java but it takes a little more effort. Remember the **round()** method in the <u>Math</u> class returns a whole number, not one with two decimals. To round in Java we can use the following code:

1. Multiply by 100 to move the decimal two positions to the right:

```
payment = payment * 100;
17057.724306813628
```

2. Call **Math.round()** to round to a whole number. Note that because **round()** returns a whole value as data type `long`, we recast it to `float`:

```
roundedPayment = (float) Math.round(payment);
  17058
```

3. Divide by 100 to move the decimal back to the left:

```
roundedPayment = roundedPayment / 100;
  170.58
```

To simplify Java rounding, we can put this code in a method named `roundOff()` and then call it whenever we wish to have a value rounded to two decimal positions. We design this method to receive a double value, round it to two decimal positions and return a `float` value. In fact, we will use this method a little later in Chapter 7 when we develop a more complete amortization program for Community National Bank. A little exercise for you here is to rewrite **roundOff()** to accept and return `long` values.

```
// roundOff method          method returns a float value
static public float roundOff (double value)
                                 method receives a double value
  {
    value = value * 100;
```

```
    // move decimal 2 places to right
    // Math.round returns long - recast to float
    float roundedValue = (float) Math.round(value);
    roundedValue = roundedValue / 100;
    // move decimal back left return roundedValue;
    // return roundedValue to calling program
} // end roundOff
```
MathClassDemo.java in Listing 5.6 demonstrates these computations.

Listing 5.6: `MathClassDemo.java`

```
// Demonstrate Use of Math class
// MathClassDemo.java
public class MathClassDemo
{
    public static void main(String args[])
    {
        // declare variables
        float balance = 1000F;
        float apr = .08F;
        int months = 6;
        double payment;
        payment = (balance*(apr/12))/(1-1/Math.pow((1+apr/
            12), months));
        System.out.println ("Payment = " + payment);
        System.out.println ("Rounded Payment = " + roundOff
            (payment));
    } // end main
    // roundOff method
    static public float roundOff (double value)
    {
        value = value * 100;
        // move decimal 2 places to right
        // Math.round returns long — recast to float
        float roundedValue = (float) Math.round(value);
        roundedValue = roundedValue / 100;
        // move decimal left two return roundedValue;
```

```
   } // end roundOff
} // end MathClassDemo.java
```

The output from the program is:

```
Payment = 170.57724306813628
Rounded Payment = 170.58
```

THE NumberFormat CLASS

COBOL uses an edit picture clause to format numeric data for display. This picture clause contains edit characters such as $, Z, 0, to control the appearance of the edited value. Given the PAYMENT from the previous section, we format it to currency by coding an edit field (EDITED-PAYMENT) containing the appropriate edit characters, then move PAYMENT to EDITED-PAYMENT.

```
01 EDITED-PAYMENT PIC $$,$$9.99.
MOVE PAYMENT TO EDITED-PAYMENT
DISPLAY "EDITED-PAYMENT =", EDITED-PAYMENT
```

The output is:

```
EDITED-PAYMENT = $170.58
```

In keeping with the spirit of OO however, Java uses methods in the appropriately named class NumberFormat, to format numerical data. The NumberFormat class is a member of the java.text package and it gives us several useful methods for formatting numerical data. Incidentally, this class also works for different countries by specifying locale. See the Java API Help documentation for the specifics. Here, we will demonstrate two of these methods: one for currency, and one for commas.

In the previous example, we had a payment value of 170.58. If we wish to have this value displayed in currency format (with a dollar sign $) we can use the NumberFormat class. Similarly, if we have another value, say 1234.56 that we wish to have displayed with a comma as 1,234.56, we again can use the NumberFormat class.

There are two steps required to convert our payment amount to currency ($170.58):

1. Create a *currency* object of NumberFormat using the class method **getCurrencyInstance()**:

   ```
   NumberFormat currencyFormat = NumberFormat.
     getCurrencyInstance();
   ```

2. Call the **format()** method in the new object to convert payment to a formatted String with a leading dollar sign:

   ```
   String formattedPayment = currencyFormat.
     format(payment);
   ```
   ──── Variable holding the value 170.58

   The String object formattedPayment now contains $170.58.

   We can also use NumberFormat to format numbers with commas, but without a dollar sign. Again, there are two steps:

1. Create an object of type NumberFormat using the class method **getInstance()**.

   ```
   NumberFormat numberFormat = NumberFormat.
   getInstance();
   ```

2. Call the **format()** method to convert a number to a formatted String with commas inserted:

   ```
   String formattedNumber = numberFormat.format(1234.56);
   ```
   ──── We can use a variable or a literal value

   The String object formattedNumber now contains 1,234.56.

   Listing 5.7 (NumberFormatDemo.java) demonstrates several of the formatting methods in NumberFormat.

Listing 5.7: `NumberFormatDemo.java`

```
// demonstrate methods in the NumberFormat class
// NumberFormatDemo.java
import java.text.*;
public class NumberFormatDemo
{
   public static void main(String args[])
```

```
    {
        // demonstrate currency format
        NumberFormat currencyFormat = NumberFormat.
          getCurrencyInstance();
        String currencyNumber = currencyFormat.
          format(123456.78);
        System.out.println ("currencyNumber = " +
          currencyNumber);
        // demonstrate comma format
        NumberFormat numberFormat = NumberFormat.
          getInstance();
        String commaNumber = numberFormat.format
          (123456.78);
        System.out.println ("commaNumber = " +
          commaNumber);
        // demonstrate percent format
        NumberFormat percentFormat = NumberFormat.
          getPercentInstance();
        String percentNumber = percentFormat.format(0.78);
        System.out.println ("percentNumber = " +
          percentNumber);
        // demonstrate decimal format
        DecimalFormat decimalFormat = new
          DecimalFormat("##,##0.00");
        String decimalNumber = decimalFormat.format
          (123456.7890);
        System.out.println ("decimalNumber = " +
          decimalNumber);
    } // end main
} // end NumberFormatDemo.java
```

The program output is:

```
currencyNumber = $123,456.78
commaNumber = 123,456.78
percentNumber = 78%
decimalNumber = 123,456.79
```

Note that the decimal format forces rounding for us.

SUMMARY OF KEY POINTS IN CHAPTER 5

1. Java uses *exceptions* as a tool to deal with errors and other important conditions that occur while our program is running. An exception is an object that contains information about the condition that caused the exception to be created. We can use the existing exception classes or define our own custom exceptions. We use the Java `try-catch` structure to execute code that can cause an exception.

2. Java has six numeric data types. Four of these (`int`, `short`, `long`, and `byte`) contain whole numbers and two (`float` and `double`) allow decimal positions. We must explicitly *cast* to convert data types from one to another whenever truncation may occur.

3. In addition to the primitive data types, Java has classes for each of these. These classes are called *wrapper* classes because they wrap an object around the data. These classes provide various methods to access and convert the data.

4. In addition to the standard add, subtract, multiply, and divide arithmetic operators, Java includes modulus, increment, decrement, and assignment operators.

5. The Math class extends Java's computation capability beyond the basic arithmetic operations. These methods include **pow()** to raise a value to a power, **round()** to return the closest integer value to the argument, and **floor()** to return a truncated value. Several of the Math class methods have similar COBOL intrinsic functions.

6. The NumberFormat class gives us tools to format numerical data by inserting commas and adding dollar signs.

CHAPTER 6

Decision Making

OBJECTIVES

In this chapter you will study:

- Conditions;
- Logical operators;
- if...else structure;
- Case structure;
- Java switch; and
- Java break.

In this chapter you will learn how to implement the selection and case structure using Java. You will see how to write if and switch statements. Java and COBOL if statements are very similar and therefore straightforward. However, switch is a distant cousin of the COBOL EVALUATE verb and has some similarities, but it also has many important differences, which will be discussed and illustrated in this chapter.

We will first examine the Java logical operators, conditions, and the if statement. This discussion includes the emulation of COBOL condition names using Java. Next we present the switch statement and explain its use. The chapter concludes with the development of a new method, **computeServiceCharge()**, for <u>CheckingAccount</u>. This method is first written using nested if statements, then written again using switch.

The chapter assumes you understand the following:

COBOL
 Condition names
 Logical operators
 `IF-ELSE-END-IF`
 `EVALUATE`
 `CONTINUE`
Java
 OO concepts (Chapter 2)
 Java program structure (Chapter 3)
 Defining data (Chapter 4)
 Computation (Chapter 5)

SERVICE CHARGES AT COMMUNITY NATIONAL BANK

The Community National Bank system computes a service charge for each checking account each month. The amount of the service charge is based on the type of account and the minimum balance in the account during the month.

 CNB has three types of checking accounts: regular, business and thrifty. The regular accounts are the most common and provide standard checking account services. The service charge for regular accounts is waived if the minimum balance is $500 or more, but is $5.00 otherwise. The service charge for business accounts is $6.00 if the minimum balance is $1000 or more, $8.00 if the minimum balance is $500 to $999.99, and $10.00 if less than $500. Thrifty checking accounts are not charged a service fee—instead customers purchase their checks from the bank.

 The decision rules for CNB are shown in Table 6.1. In this chapter we will design and write the Java code to compute the monthly service charge for each type of checking account.

THE `if` STATEMENT

The COBOL `IF` statement evaluates a *condition* then selects statements to execute depending on whether the condition is true or false. A COBOL condition is simply an expression that evaluates to either true or false. Java `if` statements look a lot like their COBOL counterparts, but Java programmers sometimes

TABLE 6.1. CNB Service Charge Calculations

Type of Account	Minimum Balance	Service Charge
Regular	500.00 or more	None
	less than 500.00	5.00
Business	1,000.00 or more	6.00
	500.00 to 999.99	8.00
	less than 500.00	10.00
Thrifty	None	None

use the term *logical expression* instead of *condition*. A logical expression is a combination of logical operators, variables, and values that evaluate to a boolean value—true or false.

Some of the Java logical operators are the same as in COBOL; however, others are quite different. For example, Java's LESS THAN (<), LESS THAN OR EQUAL TO (<=), GREATER THAN (>), and GREATER THAN OR EQUAL TO (>=) operators are identical to COBOL's, although Java lacks the spelled-out versions that we have in COBOL. Notably different are the EQUAL TO (==), OR (||), AND (&&), and NOT (!) operators used by Java.

NOTES

1. The Java EQUAL TO operator is two equal signs (==), not one (=).
2. The single symbol (=) is the Java assignment operator.
3. NOT EQUAL is denoted (!=) instead of (!==).
4. Java does not recognize the often used (<>) to mean NOT EQUAL TO.

Table 6.2 recaps the Java logical operators.

Just like in COBOL, the Java if statement evaluates a logical expression then executes statements depending on whether the expression is true or false. The primary difference between the two is:

1. Java requires the logical expression to be enclosed in parentheses.
2. Java uses a semicolon to terminate the statement to be executed.

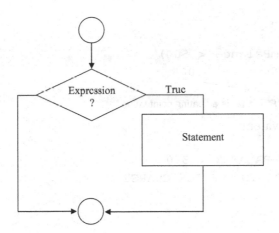

The structure of the Java if statement is:

```
if (logical expression)
    statement;                    Enclose the condition in parentheses

                        Terminate with a semicolon
```

COBOL Equivalent:

```
IF condition
statement
END-IF.
```

TABLE 6.2. Java Logical Operators	
Operator	Function
&&	AND
==	EQUAL TO
>	GREATER THAN
>=	GREATER THAN OR EQUAL TO
<	LESS THAN
<=	LESS THAN OR EQUAL TO
!	NOT
!=	NOT EQUAL TO
||	OR

A Java example is:

```
if (minimumBalance < 500)
   serviceCharge = 5.00F;
```

"*F*" indicates a floating point value

COBOL Equivalent:

```
IF MINIMUM-BALANCE < 500
   MOVE 5.00 TO SERVICE-CHARGE
END-IF.
```

USING THE else CLAUSE

We can also use the else clause with Java, similar to COBOL:

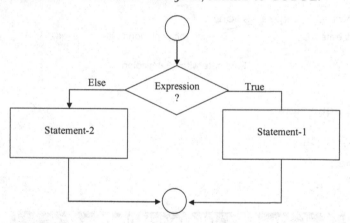

The structure of the Java if...else is:

```
if (logical expression)
   statement-1;
else
   statement-2;
```

COBOL Equivalent:

```
IF condition
   Statement-1
ELSE
   Statement-2
END-IF.
```

A Java example is:

```
if (minimumBalance < 500)
   serviceCharge = 5.00F;
else
   serviceCharge = 0.00F;
```

COBOL Equivalent:

```
IF MINIMUM-BALANCE < 500
MOVE 5.00 TO SERVICE-CHARGE
ELSE
MOVE 0.00 TO SERVICE-CHARGE
END-IF.
```

Also, like COBOL, Java can execute more than one statement based on a condition. When there is more than one statement to execute, we place the statements in a *block* using braces ({}). Notice that the braces are needed only if you want to execute more than one statement.

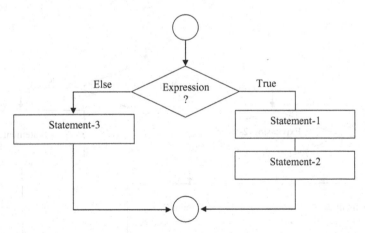

For example:

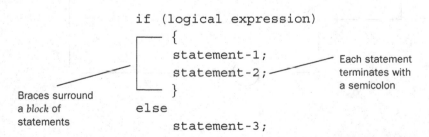

COBOL Equivalent:

```
IF condition
   statement-1
   statement-2
ELSE
   statement-3
END-IF.
```

NESTED if STATEMENTS

Just like with COBOL, we can write nested if statements using Java. Notice that we do not place a semicolon after the Java expressions.

Like COBOL, the Java compiler ignores indentation. We use it to improve the readability of our code.

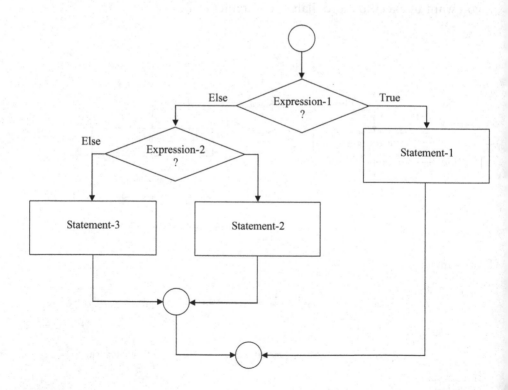

The structure of the Java nested `if` is:

```
if (logical expression-1)
   statement-1;
else
   if (logical expression-2)
      statement-2;
   else
      statement-3;
```

COBOL Equivalent:

```
IF condition-1
   statement-1
ELSE
   IF condition-2
      statement-2
   ELSE
      statement-3
   END-IF
END-IF.
```

WRITING COMPOUND CONDITIONS

We can also write compound conditions using Java's AND (`&&`) and OR (`||`) logical operators.

```
if (expression-1 && expression-2)
   statement;
```

COBOL Equivalent:

```
IF condition-1 AND condition-2
   statement
END-IF.
```

```
if (expression-1 || expression-2)
statement;
```

COBOL Equivalent:

```
IF condition-1 OR condition-2
   statement
END-IF.
```

NOTES

1. Both COBOL and Java include the reserved word CONTINUE; however, they have completely different usage.
2. The COBOL CONTINUE is used in an IF statement to transfer control to the next scope terminator (END-IF).
3. The Java continue is used in loops (while, do, and for) to terminate the current iteration and begin the next. The Java continue is discussed more thoroughly in Chapter 7 on looping.

JAVA'S CONDITIONAL OPERATOR

Java has a conditional operator that enables us to write a simple if statement using shorthand. Its structure is:

if expression true, store this value in the variable

if expression false, store this value in the variable

```
variable = logical expression ? value-1 : value-2;
```

The equivalent Java if statement is:

```
if (logical expression)
   variable = value-1;
else
   variable = value-2;
```

For example, we could write the service charge logic for a regular account as:

```
serviceCharge = minimumBalance < 500 ? 5.00F : 0.00F;
```

instead of using the if...else: ? follows the   : separates the
                                  condition   two values

```
if (minimumBalance < 500)
   serviceCharge = 5.00F;
else
   serviceCharge = 0.00F;
```

Notice that a question mark (?) follows the condition and a colon (:) separates the two values.

Use caution writing the conditional operator. Although it is a coding shortcut, it may be more difficult to read than the more familiar if statement.

CONDITION NAMES

Java does not have condition names as COBOL does. However, we can use boolean variables to emulate condition names in some situations.

Let's assume the Community National Bank has assigned checking account type codes as follows:

Code	Account Type
1	regular account
2	business account
3	thrifty account

If we were writing in COBOL, we could code these condition names as:

```
05 ACCOUNT-TYPE   PIC 9(1).
   88 REGULAR-ACCOUNT    VALUE 1.
   88 BUSINESS-ACCOUNT   VALUE 2.
   88 THRIFTY-ACCOUNT    VALUE 3.
```

Recall that in the Java language we declare variables, then either assign values at declaration time or assign values later. Also, recall that boolean variables contain only *true* or *false* values. For example, let's declare checking account type as integer:

```
int accountType;
```

Next, let's declare `boolean` variables for each type of account:

```
boolean regularAccount, businessAccount, thriftyAccount;
```

Remember, this code does not assign values to these variables; it only declares them for later reference. Also, since these are `boolean` variables, they may be assigned only *true* or *false* values. We then assign *true* or *false* values to these variables and interrogate them with the following Java code:

Only one of these variables will be set to true— the other two will be false.

```
regularAccount = (accountType == 1);
businessAccount = (accountType == 2);
thriftyAccount = (accountType == 3);
if (regularAccount)
      doSomething();
```

NOTES

1. COBOL condition names are set to *true* or *false* as values are stored in the field associated with the 88 level. The COBOL condition value is *dynamically* assigned.
2. Java DOES NOT automatically reassign values to `boolean` operators as their related variables change values. The `boolean` values must be explicitly reassigned each time a new value is stored in the related variable. In the above code, each time a new value is stored in accountType, we must reassign values to the three `boolean` variables: `regularAccount`, `businessAccount`, and `thriftyAccount`.

COMPUTING THE SERVICE CHARGE WITH `if` STATEMENTS

Next we will develop the code to compute the service charge using nested `if` statements. Let's first write the code in COBOL.

Listing 6.1: COBOL Service Charge Computation Using IF Statements

```
05 ACCOUNT-TYPE   PIC 9(1).
   88 REGULAR-ACCOUNT   VALUE 1.
   88 BUSINESS-ACCOUNT   VALUE 2.
   88 THRIFTY-ACCOUNT   VALUE 3.
05 SERVICE-CHARGE   PIC 9(2)V99.
05 MINIMUM-BALANCE   PIC S9(5)V99.
COMPUTE-SERVICE-CHARGE.
   IF REGULAR-ACCOUNT
      IF MINIMUM-BALANCE < 500
         MOVE 5.00 TO SERVICE-CHARGE
      ELSE
         MOVE ZERO TO SERVICE-CHARGE
      END-IF
   ELSE
      IF BUSINESS-ACCOUNT
   IF MINIMUM-BALANCE < 500
      MOVE 10.00 TO SERVICE-CHARGE
   ELSE
      IF MINIMUM-BALANCE < 1000
         MOVE 8.00 TO SERVICE-CHARGE
      ELSE
         MOVE 6.00 TO SERVICE-CHARGE
      END-IF
   END-IF
   ELSE
      MOVE ZERO TO SERVICE-CHARGE
   END-IF
END-IF.
```

Next, let's write the equivalent code using Java in the development of the **computeServiceCharge()** method. We first need to add the instance variable *accountType* to CheckingAccount. This new attribute is added to the class diagram shown in Figure 6.1.

The Java code for *accountType* is added to CheckingAccount.java immediately after the definition of *minimumBalance*:

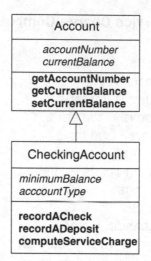

FIGURE 6.1. *Account* and *CheckingAccount* with *accountType*.

```
public class CheckingAccount extends Account
// superclass is account
{ // class variable
private float minimumBalance; // private limits
                              // access to this class
protected int accountType; // 1 is regular,
                           // 2 is business, 3 thrifty
```

Listing 6.2 below shows the complete **computeServiceCharge()** using if statements.

Listing 6.2: ComputeServiceCharge method Using if Statements

```
1. public float computeServiceCharge ()
2. {
3.    float serviceCharge;
4.    // declare and assign values to the boolean
      // variables
5.    boolean regularAccount = (accountType == 1);
6.    boolean businessAccount = (accountType == 2);
7.    boolean thriftyAcount = (accountType == 3);
8.    // compute the service charge
9.    if (regularAccount)
```

```
10.       if (minimumBalance < 500)
11.           serviceCharge = 5.00F;
12.       else
13.           serviceCharge = 0.00F;
14.    else
15.           if (businessAccount)
16.           if (minimumBalance < 500)
17.             serviceCharge = 10.00F;
18.           else
19.             if (minimumBalance < 1000)
20.                 serviceCharge = 8.00F;
21.             else
22.                 serviceCharge = 6.00F;
23.           else // thrifty account
24.             serviceCharge = 0.00F;
25.    return serviceCharge;
26. } // end of computeServiceCharge
```

NOTES

1. This method will be executed each time we want to compute the service charge for an account. Therefore, the assignment statements at lines 5 through 7 will be executed, and one of the `boolean` variables will be set to `true`, depending on the account type code contained in the variable *accountType*.
2. We could use logical expressions such as (`accountType` = 1) instead of the `boolean` variables.
3. The "F" at the end of lines 11, 13, 17, 20, 22, and 24 indicate the value is being placed in a floating-point variable.
4. Line 25 returns the computed service charge to the calling program.
5. Like COBOL, Java doesn't care at all whether we indent nested `if` statements; however, the indentation greatly improves the code's readability.

CASE STRUCTURE: COBOL EVALUATE & JAVA `switch`

The case structure is a multiple-direction decision that can often replace nested `if` statements. The case structure is implemented in COBOL with the EVALUATE verb and in Java with the `switch` statement.

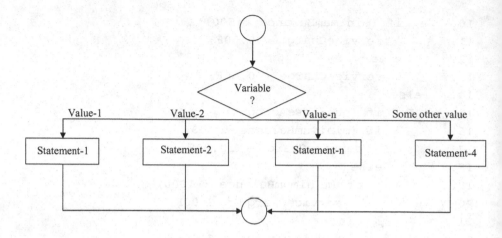

The general form of the Java switch is:

no semicolon

the body of switch is
enclosed in braces

a colon follows each
case value clause

```java
switch (variable)
{
  case value-1: statement-1;
     break;
  case value-2: statement-2;
     break;
  case value-n: statement-n;
     break;
  default: statement-4;
}
```

the body of switch is enclosed in braces

COBOL Equivalent:

```cobol
EVALUATE variable
   WHEN value-1 statement-1
   WHEN value-2 statement-2
   WHEN value-n statement-n
   WHEN OTHER statement-4
END-EVALUATE.
```

NOTES

The COBOL EVALUATE statement has some subtle but important differences from the Java switch statement:

1. COBOL can evaluate either a logical expression (EVALUATE TRUE) or the contents of a variable (EVALUATE ACCOUNT-TYPE). Java can only evaluate the contents of a variable that must be type integer or character (switch (accountType)).

2. When COBOL detects a matching value, the statements following the WHEN are executed, then control is transferred to the END-EVALUATE scope terminator. Java requires the use of the keyword break to transfer control to the end of the switch statement. If break is omitted, Java will continue to execute case statements following the one where the match occurred.

3. The values we specify in the Java switch following the keyword case, must be ordinal. That is, they must consist of ordinal data from a list such as integers and letters of the alphabet. In contrast, we can write any logical expression following the WHEN in the COBOL EVALUATE statement.

COMPUTING THE SERVICE CHARGE USING SWITCH

Next we will develop the code to compute the service charge using the case structure. Let's first write the code in COBOL.

Listing 6.3: COBOL Service Charge Computation Using EVALUATE

```
05 ACCOUNT-TYPE   PIC 9(1).
   88 REGULAR-ACCOUNT    VALUE 1.
   88 BUSINESS-ACCOUNT   VALUE 2.
   88 THRIFTY-ACCOUNT    VALUE 3.
05 SERVICE-CHARGE   PIC 9(2)V99.
05 MINIMUM-BALANCE   PIC S9(5)V99.
```

```
COMPUTE-SERVICE-CHARGE.
   EVALUATE TRUE
   WHEN REGULAR-ACCOUNT
   IF MINIMUM-BALANCE < 500
   MOVE 5.00 TO SERVICE-CHARGE
   ELSE
   MOVE ZERO TO SERVICE-CHARGE
   END-IF
   WHEN BUSINESS-ACCOUNT
   IF MINIMUM-BALANCE < 500
   MOVE 10.00 TO SERVICE-CHARGE
   ELSE
   IF MINIMUM-BALANCE < 1000
   MOVE 8.00 TO SERVICE-CHARGE
   ELSE
   MOVE 6.00 TO SERVICE-CHARGE
   END-IF
   END-IF
   WHEN THRIFTY-ACCOUNT
   MOVE ZERO TO SERVICE-CHARGE
   END-EVALUATE.
```

Notes

1. This code could be improved using nested EVALUATE statements:

```
COMPUTE-SERVICE-CHARGE.
EVALUATE TRUE
   WHEN REGULAR-ACCOUNT
   EVALUATE MINIMUM-BALANCE
   WHEN < 500 MOVE 5.00 TO SERVICE-CHARGE
   WHEN OTHER MOVE ZERO TO SERVICE-CHARGE
   END-EVALUATE
   WHEN BUSINESS-ACCOUNT
   EVALUATE MINIMUM-BALANCE
   WHEN < 500 MOVE 10.00 TO SERVICE-CHARGE
   WHEN < 1000 MOVE 8.00 TO SERVICE-CHARGE
   WHEN OTHER MOVE 6.00 TO SERVICE-CHARGE
   END-EVALUATE
```

```
WHEN THRIFTY-ACCOUNT
   MOVE ZERO TO SERVICE-CHARGE
END-EVALUATE
```

2. Although we can write nested switch statements in Java, we cannot use switch to test for relational conditions such as (minimumBalance < 500). We can only use switch to test for *specific* ordinal values of an integer or character variable. switch does not provide us with relational expressions such as <, <=, >, or >=.

Next, let's rewrite **computeServiceCharge()** using the Java switch statement:

Listing 6.4: Java Service Charge Computation Using switch

```
1. public float computeServiceCharge ()
2. {
3.    float serviceCharge;
4.    switch (accountType)
5.    {
6.       case 1: // regular account
7.          if (minimumBalance < 500)
8.             serviceCharge = 5.00F;
9.          else
10.            serviceCharge = 0.00F;
11.            break;
12.       case 2: // business account
13.          if (minimumBalance < 500)
14.             serviceCharge = 10.00F;
15.          else
16.             if (minimumBalance < 1000)
17.                serviceCharge = 8.00F;
18.             else
19.                serviceCharge = 6.00F;
20.                break;
21.       case 3: // thrifty account
22.             serviceCharge = 0.00F;
23.    } // end of switch
24.    return serviceCharge;
25. } // end computeServiceCharge
```

Notes

1. The placement of the semicolon(;), colon (:), and braces ({}) are critical in the `switch` statement:
   - There is NOT a semicolon following `switch` (see line 4):
     `switch (accountType)`
   - Each `case` terminates with a colon, not a semicolon:
     `case 1:`
   - The body of the `switch` block is enclosed in braces.
2. Notice the braces ({ and }) at lines 5 and 23. These are required and indicate the boundaries of the `switch` block.
3. The `break` statements at lines 11 and 20 transfer execution to the end of the `switch` block at line 23.
4. As previously mentioned, we cannot replace the `if` statements here with nested `switch` statements. Java permits us to test only for specific ordinal values. For example, we cannot use `switch` with an expression like `minimumBalance < 500`.
5. Good programming practices would require us to code a default case to cover an account type other than 1, 2, or 3. To keep the examples brief, we have omitted the default here.

Summary of Key Points in Chapter 6

1. The COBOL and Java logical operators have both similarities and differences:

Java	COBOL
&&	AND
==	EQUAL TO, =
>	GREATER THAN, >
>=	GREATER THAN OR EQUAL TO, >=
<	LESS THAN, <
<=	LESS THAN OR EQUAL TO, <=
!	NOT
!=	NOT EQUAL TO, NOT =, <>
||	OR

2. The COBOL and Java if statements are very similar:

Java	COBOL
A. if (logical expression) statement;	IF condition statement END-IF.
B. if (logical expression) statement-1; else statement-2;	IF condition statement-1 ELSE statement-2 END-IF.
C. if (logical expression) {statement-1; statement-2;} else statement-3;	IF condition statement-1 statement-2 ELSE statement-3 END-IF.

D. if (logical
    expression-1)
   statement-1;
else
  if (logical
   expression-2)
   statement-2;
   else
   statement-3;
	IF condition-1
	   statement-1
	ELSE
	   IF condition-2
	   statement-2
	ELSE
	   statement-3
	   END-IF
	END-IF.

E. if (expression-1 && expression-2) statement;	IF condition-1 AND condition-2 statement END-IF.
F. if (expression-1 || expression-2) statement;	IF condition-1 OR condition-2 statement END-IF.

3. We can emulate COBOL condition names in Java

```
regularAccount = (accountType == 1);
businessAccount = (accountType == 2);
thriftyAccount = (accountType == 3);
if (regularAccount)
    doSomething;
```

4. There are major differences between COBOL's EVALUATE and Java's switch statements:

   - COBOL can evaluate either a boolean condition (EVALUATE TRUE) or the contents of a variable (EVALUATE ACCOUNT-TYPE). Java can only evaluate the contents of a variable that must be type integer or character (switch accountType).
   - When COBOL detects a matching value, the statements following the WHEN are executed, then control is transferred to the END-EVALUATE scope terminator. Java requires the use of the keyword break to transfer control to the end of the switch statement. If break is omitted, Java will continue to execute case statements following the one where the match occurred.
   - The values we can specify in the Java switch following the keyword case must be ordinal. That is, they must consist of ordinal data from a list such as integers and letters of the alphabet. In contrast, we can write any logical expression following the WHEN in the COBOL EVALUATE statement.

5. Java's conditional operator enables us to write abbreviated if statements. The shorthand code

```
serviceCharge = minimumBalance < 500 ? 5.00F : 0.00F;
```

can replace the if-else:

```
if (minimumBalance < 500)
    serviceCharge = 5.00F;
else
    serviceCharge = 0.00F;
```

CHAPTER 7

Loops

OBJECTIVES

In this chapter you will study:

- `while` loop;
- `do` loop;
- `for` loop;
- Nested loops;
- `break` statement; and
- `continue` statement.

This chapter shows you how to write Java loops. You will learn how to write loops that mirror the familiar COBOL `PERFORM` statement including the `PERFORM-UNTIL`, `PERFORM-VARYING-UNTIL` and `PERFORM-VARYING-UNTIL-AFTER`. You will see that Java has three different types of loops: `while`, `do`, and `for`. We will use each of these to duplicate the work done by the COBOL `PERFORM` statement. In addition, we will review loops that test for the terminating condition at the beginning and at the end of the loop. We will also demonstrate writing nested loops in Java.

The chapter begins with the simple COBOL `PERFORM-UNTIL` statement and shows you how to accomplish the same thing in Java. Then we work with

the PERFORM-VARYING-UNTIL and finally the PERFORM-VARYING-UNTIL-
AFTER statement. Working programs are developed to illustrate the Java loop
statements in action. At the end of the chapter, we design and develop a small
program for the Community Naitonal Bank to compute a loan amortization,
using some of the Java looping statements.

   This chapter assumes you understand the following:

COBOL:
   Perform-until
   Inline perform (COBOL-85)
   Perform-varying-until
   Perform-varying-until-after
   With test after (COBOL-85)
Java:
   OO concepts (Chapter 2)
   Java program structure (Chapter 3)
   Defining data (Chapter 4)
   Arithmetic (Chapter 5)
   Decision making (Chapter 6)

Loop Structure

We write program loops to repeat a sequence of instructions. In COBOL we use
the PERFORM statement and its variations to construct loops. In Java we have
three different statements to choose from: while, do, and for. Regardless
of the loop statement employed, or the language used for that matter, all loops
are similar.

   We write loops that test for the terminating condition either at the beginning of the loop (*pre-test*) or at the end of the loop (*post-test*). The main
difference between pre-test and post-test loops is that the post-test loop will
always execute the loop statements at least once. The pre-test loop, however,
will not execute the loop statements if the terminating condition is true when
execution begins. The flowcharts in Figure 7.1 map these two general loop
structures.

The COBOL Perform Statement

The COBOL language has several variations of the PERFORM statement that
are used to code loops. The COBOL-74 PERFORM loop was always a pre-test.

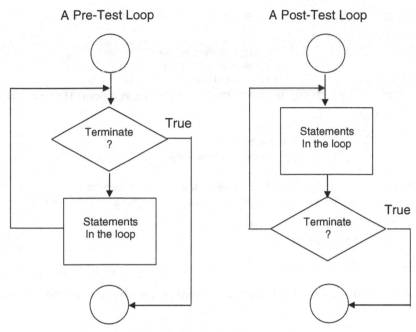

FIGURE **7.1. Loop structures.**

The following lists three of the more frequently used COBOL-74 PERFORM statements that are used to write loops:

COBOL-74

```
PERFORM paragraph_name number_of_times
PERFORM paragraph_name UNTIL terminate_condition
PERFORM paragraph_name VARYING variable-name
   FROM initial_value BY increment_value
   UNTIL terminate_condition
```

The paragraph_name referenced in these PERFORM statements contain the code to be executed in the loop. In other words, the paragraph referenced by paragraph_name contains the body of the loop.

COBOL-85 introduced the *inline* PERFORM and its corresponding scope terminator, END-PERFORM, which allows us to write a loop without the need for a separate paragraph. We simply sandwich the loop statements between the PERFORM and the END-PERFORM. COBOL-85 also gave us the option of specifying either a pre-test or post-test loop structure by including the WITH

TEST BEFORE (pre-test) or WITH TEST AFTER (post-test) clause.

```
                        The WITH TEST BEFORE
                       / is the default and is generally
    COBOL-85          /  not explicitly coded
    PERFORM WITH TEST BEFORE UNTIL terminate_condition
    loop statements
    END-PERFORM
                            The WITH TEST AFTER
                           / indicates a post-test loop
                          /
    PERFORM WITH TEST AFTER VARYING variable-name
        FROM initial_value BY increment_value
        UNTIL terminate_condition
        loop statements
    END-PERFORM
```

We will use the COBOL-85 PERFORM syntax for the remaining examples here.

THE JAVA while STATEMENT

The Java while statement is used to write pre-test loops, similar to the familiar COBOL PERFORM-UNTIL.

The basic structure of the while is:

```
    while(boolean_expression)
    {                       the loop terminates when
        statements          this expression is false
    }
          In keeping with Java syntax, braces mark
          the beginning and end of the loop body
```

COBOL Equivalent:

```
    PERFORM UNTIL condition
        statements
    END-PERFORM.            The COBOL loop terminates
                            when this condition is true.
```

NOTES

1. The COBOL >, >=, <, and <= operators are identical in Java.
2. However the *equal to*, *not equal to*, *and*, *or*, and *not* operators are totally
   different:

Operator	COBOL	Java
Equal to	=	==
Not equal to	NOT =	!=
And	AND	&&
Or	OR	||
Not	NOT	!

To illustrate, let's use a `while` loop to print the numbers 1 through 5. First,
we initialize our number to 1, then loop to print and increment the number.
We want the loop to terminate after our number becomes greater than 5. The
Java code is:

keep looping while this condition is true

```
int number = 1;
while (number <= 5)
{
    System.out.println (number);
    number = number + 1;
}
```

Within the loop we print number
and then add 1 to it

The body of the loop is enclosed
in braces

COBOL Equivalent:

```
MOVE 1 TO NUMBER
PERFORM UNTIL NUMBER > 5
    DISPLAY NUMBER
    ADD 1 TO NUMBER
    END-PERFORM.
```

NOTES

If the braces are omitted, Java **assumes a one statement loop**. This example, without braces will create **an endless loop**, because the statement

```
number = number + 1;
```

will not be part of the loop and number will not be incremented within the loop.

Another loop example is to determine the number of years it will take for the balance in a savings account to double in value, given a fixed rate of interest and assuming we make a fixed deposit at the end of every year. Let's first declare our variables and assign values. We use a beginning balance of $1,000, an annual interest rate of 5.0%, and an annual deposit of $100.

```
// declare variables
float initialbalance = 1000F; // initial account balance
float annualDeposit = 100F;  // amount of annual deposit
float apr = 0.05F; // annual percentage rate of interest
float currentBalance;  // the running account balance
int numberOfYears; // number of years to double in value
```

Before beginning the loop, we assign the initial account balance to cur-rentBalance and initialize the numberOfYears variable to zero.

```
currentBalance = initialBalance;
numberOfYears = 0;
```

Then at the end of each year (each loop) we compute the interest earned during the year, add the interest to the current balance, then add the annual deposit amount to the current balance. The statement to do this computation is:

```
currentBalance = currentBalance * (1 + apr) +
  annualDeposit;
```

We then write the loop:

The loop terminates when `currentBalance`
exceeds twice the `initialBalance`

```
while (currentBalance <= (2 * initialBalance))
```

Compute the new balance &
increment `numberOfYears`

```
{
   currentBalance = currentBalance * (1 + apr) +
     annualDeposit;
   numberOfYears = numberOfYears + 1;
   System.out.println ("Year" + numberOfYears +
   Math.round (currentBalance));
}
```

The body of the loop is
enclosed between braces

Print the year number
and balance at end of
each loop (year)

Note that the loop is a pre-test loop. It will check the terminating condition before executing the loop instructions. After the loop terminates, we print the `numberOfYears` and `currentBalance`.

```
System.out.print ("In " + numberOfYears + " years");
System.out.println ("The balance will be " +
   Math.round(currentBalance));
```

We have put this code together in a small program named `WhileLoopDemo.java` (see Listing 7.1).

Listing 7.1: `WhileLoopDemo.java`

```
public class WhileLoopDemo
{
   public static void main (String args[])
   {
   float initialBalance = 1000F;
   // begin with $1,000 balance
   float annualDeposit = 100F;
   // deposit $100 end of each year
```

```
float apr = 0.05F;
// annual interest rate is 5%
float currentBalance;      // running balance
int numberOfYears;         // count number of years
// initialize currentBalance and numberOfYears
currentBalance = initialBalance;
numberOfYears = 0;
System.out.println ("Output From while Loop");
// print headings
System.out.println ("Year Balance");
// beginning of while loop
while (currentBalance <= (2 * initialBalance))
{
   currentBalance = currentBalance * (1 + apr) +
     annualDeposit;
   numberOfYears = numberOfYears + 1;
   System.out.println (numberOfYears + " " +
     Math.round(currentBalance));
} // end of while loop
System.out.print ("In " + numberOfYears + " years");
System.out.println ("the balance will be " +
   Math.round(currentBalance));
} // end of main method
} // end of WhileLoopDemo.java
```

The output from `WhileLoopDemo.java` is

```
Output From while Loop
Year Balance
1 1150
2 1308
3 1473
4 1647
5 1829
6 2020
```

```
In 6 years the balance will be 2020
```

THE JAVA do STATEMENT

The Java do statement is used to write post-test loops. We use the COBOL-85 PERFORM WITH TEST AFTER clause to code COBOL post-test loops.

The basic structure of the do is:

```
do
{____ again braces mark the beginning
       and end of the loop body

    statements
} while(boolean_expression);
```

The terminating condition is at the **end** of the do loop.
The loop terminates when this expression is **false**

COBOL Equivalent:

```
PERFORM WITH TEST AFTER
    UNTIL boolean_expression
        statements
    END-PERFORM.
```

The Java do loop is sometimes called a do-while loop because the while clause is written at the end of the loop. The do loop and while loop are similar except the while loop is pre-test and the do loop is post-test. Both terminate when the boolean expression is false.

NOTES

1. Java loops terminate when the boolean expression is **false**.
2. COBOL loops terminate when the boolean_expression is **true**.

We can use a do loop to print the numbers 1 through 5 just as we did before, and the code is quite similar. First, we initialize our number to 1, then loop to print and increment the number. We want the loop to terminate when our number becomes greater than 5. The Java code is

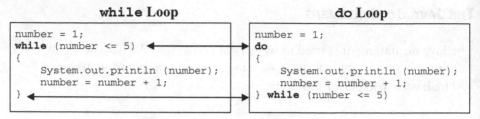

FIGURE 7.2. while loop and do loop.

```
int number = 1;
do                          Within the loop we print number and then add 1 to it
{
    System.out.println (number);
    number = number + 1;
} while (number <= 5)
```

we write the while clause at   keep looping while this
the end of the do loop   condition is true

COBOL Equivalent:

```
MOVE 1 TO NUMBER
PERFORM WITH TEST AFTER
    UNTIL NUMBER > 5
        DISPLAY NUMBER
        ADD 1 TO NUMBER
END-PERFORM.
```

Note that the loop is a post-test loop. The condition is checked after the loop instructions. In this case, the loop would have executed at least once regardless of the value of number.

When we place the while and do loops side by side you can see their similarity (Figure 7.2). The only difference is that the while loop has the while clause at the beginning and the do loop has do at the beginning and the while at the end. Notice that the terminating condition and the statements within the loop are identical.

We can easily modify the previous program, WhileLoopDemo.java, to use the do statement. We name this modified program DoLoopDemo.java. We changed five lines (all boldface), but only two, the do and while statements, impact the program's execution.

Listing 7.2: `DoLoopDemo.java`

```java
public class DoLoopDemo
{
    public static void main (String args[])
    {
        // declare variables
        float initialBalance = 1000F;
        // begin with $1,000 balance
        float annualDeposit = 100F;
        // deposit $100 end of each year
        float apr = 0.05F;
        // annual interest rate is 5%
        float currentBalance;    // running balance
        int numberOfYears;        // count number of years
        // initialize currentBalance and numberOfYears
        currentBalance = initialBalance;
        numberOfYears = 0;
        System.out.println ("Output From do Loop");
        // print headings
        System.out.println ("Year Balance");
        // beginning of do loop
        do
        {
            currentBalance = currentBalance * (1 + apr) +
                annualDeposit;
            numberOfYears = numberOfYears + 1;
            System.out.println (numberOfYears + " " +
                Math.round(currentBalance));
        } while (currentBalance <= (2 * initialBalance));
        // end of loop
        System.out.print ("In " + numberOfYears +
            " years ");
        System.out.println ("the balance will be " +
            Math.round(currentBalance));
    } // end of main method
} // end of DoLoopDemo.java
```

The output from `DoLooopDemo.java` is shown below, which is the same as the previous example.

```
Output From do Loop
Year Balance
1 1150
2 1308
3 1473
4 1647
5 1829
6 2020
In 6 years the balance will be 2020
```

THE JAVA for STATEMENT

So far we have used the Java `while` and `do` statements to write loops. These examples initialized a *loop counter* such as `number` or `numberOfYears`, and the loop included a statement to increment the counter. When we use the `while` or `do`, we are responsible for initializing and incrementing any loop counter variables used. The COBOL counterpart of the Java `while` and `do` statements is the `PERFORM-UNTIL`.

In COBOL we can use the `PERFORM-VARYING-UNTIL` statement to automatically initialize and increment loop counters for us. For example, let's again print 1 through 5, but this time let's use a `PERFORM-VARYING-UNTIL` statement.

```
PERFORM VARYING NUMBER FROM 1 BY 1
   UNTIL NUMBER > 5
      DISPLAY NUMBER
END-PERFORM.
```

This code represents a pre-test loop and is both simpler and shorter because we do not need the initialization statement (`MOVE 1 TO NUMBER`) or the increment statement (`ADD 1 TO NUMBER`).

We use the Java `for` loop to initialize and increment loop counters for us. It is a pre-test loop and its structure is:

initialize the loop counter
variable

The loop terminates when
this expression is **false**

```
for (initialize_statement; boolean_expression;
    increment_statement)
{
```

—— increment the variable   semicolons are separators

```
    statements
}
```
——braces mark the beginning and end of the loop body

COBOL Equivalent:

```
PERFORM VARYING variable-name FROM initial-value
BY increment-value UNTIL condition
    statements
END-PERFORM.
```

We can use the `for` loop to once again print the numbers 1 through 5.

we can both declare &
initialize number here

this is the same condition
we used before

add 1 to number

```
for (int number = 1; number <= 5; number = number + 1)
{
    System.out.println (number);
}
```

COBOL Equivalent:

```
PERFORM VARYING number FROM 1 BY 1 UNTIL number > 5
    DISPLAY NUMBER
END-PERFORM
```

NOTES

1. If we declare the variable number in the `for` statement, its scope is limited to this loop.
2. We can choose to declare the variable outside the loop to give it method scope.

We have again modified WhileLoopDemo.java, this time to demonstrate the for statement. We name this modified program ForLoopDemo.java. We converted the while loop to a for loop and moved the initialize and increment statements into the for statement.

Listing 7.3: ForLoopDemo.java

```
public class ForLoopDemo
{
   public static void main (String args[])
   {
     // declare variables
     float initialBalance = 1000F;
     // begin with $1,000 balance
     float annualDeposit = 100F;
     // deposit $100 end of each year
     float apr = 0.05F;
     // annual interest rate is 5%
     float currentBalance;    // running balance
     int numberOfYears;        // count number of years
     // initialize currentBalance and numberOfYears
     currentBalance = initialBalance;
     System.out.println ("Output From for Loop");
     // print headings
     System.out.println ("Year Balance");
     // beginning of for loop
     for (numberOfYears = 0; currentBalance <=
       (2 * initialBalance); numberOfYears =
         numberOfYears + 1)
     {
       currentBalance = currentBalance * (1 + apr) +
         annualDeposit;
       System.out.println (numberOfYears + " " +
         Math.round(currentBalance));
     } // end of for loop
     System.out.print ("In " + numberOfYears +
       " years ");
```

```
        System.out.println ("the balance will be " +
          Math.round(currentBalance));
    } // end of main method
} // end of ForLoopDemo.java
```

The output of `ForLoopDemo.java` is shown below, and it is the same as the previous two examples.

```
Output From for Loop
Year Balance
1 1150
2 1308
3 1473
4 1647
5 1829
6 2020
In 6 years the balance will be 2020.
```

NESTED LOOPS

As in COBOL, we can write nested loops in Java. In COBOL we can write a nested loop using two loop statements. For example:

```
PERFORM VARYING NUMBER1 FROM 1 BY 1 UNTIL NUMBER1 > 3
    PERFORM VARYING NUMBER2 FROM 1 BY 1 UNTIL NUMBER2 > 2
        DISPLAY NUMBER1, NUMBER2
    END-PERFORM
END-PERFORM.
```

This code will execute the `DISPLAY` statement 6 times and will print:

Number1	Number2
1	1
1	2
2	1
2	2
3	1
3	2

We can rewrite this nested loop using the COBOL PERFORM-VARYING-AFTER statement, which simplifies the code a little:

```
PERFORM VARYING NUMBER1 FROM 1 BY 1 UNTIL NUMBER1 > 3
    AFTER NUMBER2 FROM 1 BY 1 UNTIL NUMBER2 > 2
        DISPLAY NUMBER1, NUMBER2
END-PERFORM.
```

The DISPLAY statement again executes six times and the output is the same as before.

Although Java does not have a counterpart to COBOL's PERFORM-VARYING-AFTER statement, we can certainly simulate it by writing a loop within a loop.

```
for (int number1 = 1; number1 <= 3; number1 =
  number1 + 1)
{
    for (int number2 = 1; number2 <= 2; number2 =
      number2 + 1)
    {
        System.out.println (number1 + " " + number2);
    } // end of inner loop
} // end of outer loop
```

Similar to the COBOL example, this code will execute the **println()** method six times and will print:

Number1	Number2
1	1
1	2
2	1
2	2
3	1
3	2

Keep in mind that the scope of the variables declared in the loop is limited to the loop.

Of course we can use any combination of while, do, and for statements to construct nested loops.

JAVA break AND continue STATEMENTS

Java provides two statements to prematurely terminate or to skip a loop: break and continue. The break statement immediately terminates a loop while continue terminates only the current iteration of the loop. The break and continue statements are typically used with an if statement that tests for a condition that warrants the termination of the loop.

NOTES

1. The Java continue and COBOL continue are totally different key words.
2. Java continue terminates the current loop iteration.
3. COBOL continue goes to the scope terminator in an IF statement.

To illustrate, we can print the numbers 1 through 5 as in previous examples, but here let's skip the number 3 by using the continue statement. This code will print 1, 2, 4, and 5.

```
        int number = 1;
        while (number <=5)
        {
        if (number == 3)  // don't print the number 3
        {
        number = number + 1;
        // increment to avoid endless loop
            continue;         // continue skips to end of loop
        } // end if
        System.out.println (number);
        number = number + 1;
        } // end while
```

Now let's use the same code, but **stop** printing at 3 using the break.

```
 int number = 1;
 while (number <=5)
 {
```

```
        if (number == 3) // stop loop at 3
    ┌────── break;              // break terminates the loop
    │   System.out.println (number);
    │   number = number + 1;
    └─► } // end while
```

This code will print only 1 and 2. The statement

```
if (number == 3)
break;
```

exits the loop when number reaches 3.

PRODUCING A LOAN AMORTIZATION SCHEDULE

A loan amortization schedule gives us detailed payment information about a loan such as the payment amount and the amount of interest and principal paid each month. In this section we will develop a method to compute and display a loan amortization schedule for Community National Bank.

If we know the original loan amount (balance), the annual percentage interest rate (apr), and the loan duration expressed in number of months (months), we can calculate the monthly loan payment using the formula we developed in Chapter 5:

> apr/12 is the monthly rate

> Math.pow(x,y) returns x raised to the y power

```
payment = (balance * (apr / 12)/Math.pow ((1 - apr/12),
    months);
```

We can then use the **roundOff()** method we also developed in Chapter 5 to round the payment amount to two decimal positions.

```
payment = roundOff(payment);
```

Next, knowing the monthly payment amount, we can then compute the interest and principal paid each month over the life of the loan. We write a `while` loop to loop once for each month. `monthNumber` is our loop counter and `months` is the duration of the loan.

```
while (monthNumber <= months)
```

The interest to be paid each month will simply be the monthly interest rate applied to the remaining loan balance. Again we round the interest.

```
interestPaid = roundOff (balance * apr / 12);
```

The portion of the payment that is applied to reducing the loan amount is the payment amount less the interest paid.

```
principalPaid = payment - interestPaid;
```

The new loan balance after the payment has been made is the previous balance less the amount applied to principal.

```
balance = balance - principalPaid;
```

The complete program named `Amortizer.java` is shown in Listing 7.4.

Listing 7.4: `Amortizer.java`

```
import java.text.NumberFormat;
public class Amortizer
{
   public static void main (String args[])
   {
      // declare variables
      float balance = 1000F;
      float apr = .08F;
      int months = 6;
      float interestPaid = 0F;
      float principalPaid = 0F;
      float totalInterestPaid = 0F;
      // compute payment
      double doublePayment = (balance * (apr / 12))/
         (1 - 1 / Math.pow ((1 + apr/12), months));
      float payment = (float) doublePayment;
```

```
    // cast to float
    payment = roundOff (payment); // round to cents
    // print heading
    System.out.println ("Mo Payment Interest Principal
      Balance");
    // beginning of while loop
    int monthNumber = 1;
    while (monthNumber <= months)
    {
      interestPaid = roundOff (balance * apr / 12);
      totalInterestPaid = totalInterestPaid +
        interestPaid;

      if (monthNumber == months)
      payment = interestPaid + balance;
      principalPaid = payment - interestPaid;
      balance = roundOff(balance - principalPaid);
      // print a line
      System.out.print (" " + monthNumber);
      System.out.print (" " + payment);
      System.out.print (" " + interestPaid);
      System.out.print (" " + principalPaid);
      System.out.println (" " + balance);
      monthNumber = monthNumber + 1;
  } // end of while loop
  System.out.println ("Total Interest Paid " +
    roundOff(totalInterestPaid));
  } // end of main method
  // roundOff method
  static public float roundOff (double value)
  {
    value = value * 100;
    // move decimal 2 places to right
    // Math.round returns long - recast to float
    float roundedValue = (float) Math.round(value);
    roundedValue = roundedValue / 100;
    return roundedValue;
  } // end roundOff
} // end of Amortizer.java
```

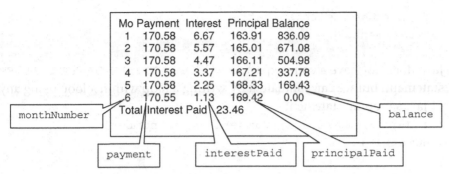

FIGURE 7.3. **Amortizer.java** output.

The program output is shown below in Figure 7.3.

A good exercise for you here is to convert Amortizer.java to a method, then write a Loan Processor program that calls the **amortizeLoan()** method. The method signature would be:

```
public void amortizeLoan (float balance, float apr,
    int months)
```

Or you could have the method to return a value such as payment if you wish.

SUMMARY OF KEY POINTS IN CHAPTER 7

1. In general there are two types of loops: *pre-test* loops test for the terminating condition at the beginning of the loop and *post-test* loops test at the end of the loop.
2. Java has three loop statements: while, do, and for. The while statement is a pre-test loop and the other two are post-test loops.
```
while(boolean_expression) // loop while this is true
{
    statements
}
do
{
    statements
} while(boolean_expression) // loop while this is true
for (initialize; boolean_expression; increment)
```

```
{ // loop while this is true
  statements
}
```

3. Java does not have a counterpart to COBOL's PERFORM-VARYING-AFTER
   statement, but we can simulate it by writing a loop within a loop using any
   of Java's looping statements.

```
for (int number1 = 1; number1 <= 3; number1 =
  number1 + 1)
{
   for (int number2 = 1; number2 <= 2; number2 =
     number2 + 1)
   {
     System.out.println (number1 + " " + number2);
   } // end of inner loop
} // end of outer loop
```

4. Java provides two statements to prematurely terminate a loop: break and
   continue. break immediately terminates a loop. continue terminates
   only the current iteration of the loop.

CHAPTER 8

Arrays

OBJECTIVES

In this chapter you will study:

- One-dimensional arrays;
- Two-dimensional arrays;
- Searching arrays; and
- Passing arrays as arguments.

This chapter shows you how to work with arrays. You will learn how to define and manipulate both single and multidimensional arrays. In this chapter, as in others, we will develop real working programs to illustrate using Java arrays.

NOTES

1. COBOL uses the terms *single-level table*; Java uses *one-dimensional array*.
2. In keeping with the spirit of Java, here we will use array and dimension.

This chapter begins with the declaration and population of one-dimensional arrays, then illustrates how to declare and populate two-dimensional arrays. The examples use both numeric and string data values.

The chapter also describes how to search an array using Java and how to pass arrays as arguments to methods.

You will see that, although internally Java treats array processing somewhat differently than COBOL, Java array handling looks a lot like COBOL table processing to the programmer. Of course, we will continue to point out significant differences between Java and COBOL and the pitfalls to avoid when writing Java from a COBOL programmer's perspective.

This chapter assumes you understand the following:

COBOL:
   Defining one & two level tables
   Initializing one & two level tables
   Table lookup techniques
   Using subscripts and indexes
   Perform-varying statement
Java:
   OO concepts (Chapter 2)
   Java program structure (Chapter 3)
   Defining data (Chapter 4)
   Decision making (Chapter 6)
   Looping (Chapter 7)

DECLARING ONE-DIMENSIONAL ARRAYS

We begin our discussion of one-dimensional arrays by looking at loan processing for the Community National Bank (CNB). Let's assume that CNB wants to track the number of new loans made during each month for the calendar year. We can accomplish this by using a one-dimensional array with 12 elements—one element for each month.

In COBOL we declare the array as:

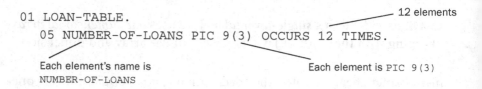

```
01 LOAN-TABLE.                                                    ┌─ 12 elements
   05 NUMBER-OF-LOANS PIC 9(3) OCCURS 12 TIMES.
```

Each element's name is   Each element is PIC 9(3)
NUMBER-OF-LOANS

This code creates a 12 element array named LOAN-TABLE, with each element a `PIC 9(3)` field named `NUMBER-OF-LOANS`. We use the COBOL OCCURS clause to tell the compiler how many elements we want to have.

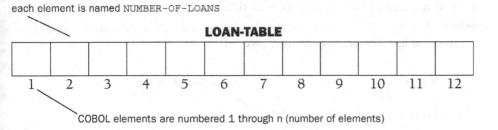

each element is named `NUMBER-OF-LOANS`

LOAN-TABLE

| 1 | 2 | 3 | 4 | 5 | 6 | 7 | 8 | 9 | 10 | 11 | 12 |

COBOL elements are numbered 1 through n (number of elements)

COBOL uses a *subscript* to indicate which element we wish to access. For example, to display the number of loans made in January we write:

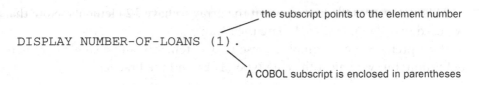

the subscript points to the element number

`DISPLAY NUMBER-OF-LOANS (1).`

A COBOL subscript is enclosed in parentheses

NOTES

1. COBOL makes a distinction between a *subscript* and an *index*. COBOL uses an index with the SEARCH verb.
2. Java does not use the term *subscript*, but instead uses the term *index*. It is used like the COBOL subscript—it specifies the element number of an array.
3. Here we will use *subscript* when discussing COBOL and *index* when dealing with Java syntax.

The declaration of an array in Java looks quite similar to the variable declarations described in Chapter 4. Our loan array would be declared as:

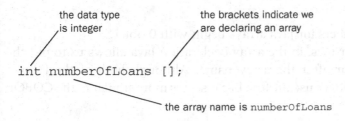

the data type is integer

the brackets indicate we are declaring an array

`int numberOfLoans [];`

the array name is `numberOfLoans`

In fact, this statement *does not* reserve memory for our array. You will notice that we did not tell the Java compiler how many elements we needed. This statement simply tells Java that we are going to create a variable named `numberOfLoans` and we will define it as an array more completely later.

To complete the array definition, we write:

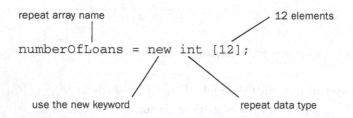

repeat array name

12 elements

```
numberOfLoans = new int [12];
```

use the new keyword

repeat data type

This statement tells Java we want the array to have 12 elements. Note that we used two statements to declare the array.

If we prefer, we can combine these two statements into a single complete definition, but we repeat the data type (`int`) and the brackets:

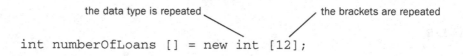

the data type is repeated

the brackets are repeated

```
int numberOfLoans [] = new int [12];
```

The Java array appears as:

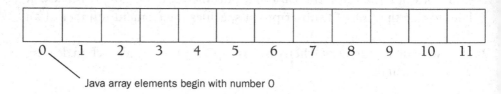

| 0 | 1 | 2 | 3 | 4 | 5 | 6 | 7 | 8 | 9 | 10 | 11 |

Java array elements begin with number 0

NOTES

1. The element numbers for Java arrays begin with 0 not 1.
2. To keep us on our toes, in the array declaration Java allows us to put the brackets **before or after** the array name. Although both of the following formats are OK, we use the first because it is more similar to the COBOL syntax:

```
datatype arrayname [] = new datatype
  [number_of_elements];
or
datatype [] arrayname = new datatype
  [number_of_elements];
```

3. The new operator suggests we are creating an object, which is exactly what happens. This fact, however, has very little impact on our array processing code. We will point out those places where we need to be aware the array is actually an object.

POPULATING ONE-DIMENSIONAL ARRAYS

There are two different ways to populate a COBOL array. We can either use the value clause in the data division or procedural statements in the procedure division to place values into the array. Here, the first example uses the value clause to establish values for the array.

```
01 NUMBER-OF-LOAN-VALUES.
   05 FILLER PIC 9(3) VALUE 39.
   05 FILLER PIC 9(3) VALUE 44.
   05 FILLER PIC 9(3) VALUE 45.
   05 FILLER PIC 9(3) VALUE 65.
   05 FILLER PIC 9(3) VALUE 72.
   05 FILLER PIC 9(3) VALUE 93.
   05 FILLER PIC 9(3) VALUE 14.
   05 FILLER PIC 9(3) VALUE 55.
   05 FILLER PIC 9(3) VALUE 67.
   05 FILLER PIC 9(3) VALUE 27.
   05 FILLER PIC 9(3) VALUE 46.
   05 FILLER PIC 9(3) VALUE 82.
01 LOAN-TABLE REDEFINES NUMBER-OF-LOAN-VALUES.
   05 NUMBER-OF-LOANS PIC 9(3) OCCURS 12 TIMES.
```

NOTES

1. This example uses COBOL-78 syntax.
2. COBOL-85 (and COBOL–2002) allow us to omit FILLER. We could write PIC 9(3) VALUE 39.

3. The REDEFINES clause allows multiple names and picture clauses to be assigned to the same data items.

To assign values to an array at execution time we can write procedure division code:

```
MOVE 39 TO NUMBER-OF-LOANS(1)
MOVE 44 TO NUMBER-OF-LOANS(2)
..etc.
```

Regardless of the population technique, the populated array now appears as:

LOAN-TABLE

39	44	45	65	72	93	14	55	67	27	46	82
1	2	3	4	5	6	7	8	9	10	11	12

The statement:

```
DISPLAY NUMBER-OF-LOANS (3)
```

will display "45," the contents of the third element—the number of loans CNB made in March.

Similar to COBOL, we can populate Java arrays either at declaration time or with procedural statements. To declare and populate the array in a single statement, we write:

```
int numberOfLoans [] = {39,44,45,65,72,93,14,55,67,27,46,82};
```

number of elements
not specified

values are enclosed
in braces & separated
by commas

don't forget
the semicolon

Notice that we omit the new operator and do not specify the number of elements when we declare and populate in the same statement. The Java compiler determines the number of elements from the data value list.

If we prefer to populate a Java array with assignment statements we would write:

remember, the first element in
a Java array is number 0!

```
numberOfLoans [0] = 39;
numberOfLoans [1] = 44;
.. etc.
```

To display the contents of an element, say the third one, using Java we can write:

parentheses surround the argument being
passed to the method **println()**

remember, use brackets for
the index, not parentheses

```
System.out.println (numberOfLoans [2]);
```

an index value of 2 points to
the *third* element of the array

This will again print "45" from the third element of the array numberOf-Loans.

CREATING STRING ARRAYS

Let's assume we want an array containing the names of the months. In COBOL we would write:

```
01 MONTH-NAME-VALUES.
   05 PIC X(36) VALUE
      'JanFebMarAprMayJunJulAugSepOctNovDec'.
01 MONTH-NAME-TABLE REDEFINES MONTH-NAME-VALUES.
   05 MONTH-NAME PIC X(3) OCCURS 12 TIMES.
```

This creates a 12 element array with each element named MONTH-NAME:

MONTH-NAME-TABLE

Jan	Feb	Mar	Apr	May	Jun	Jul	Aug	Sep	Oct	Nov	Dec
1	2	3	4	5	6	7	8	9	10	11	12

To declare and populate this array using Java we write:

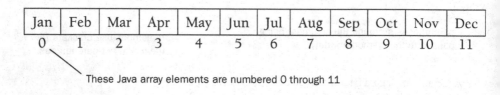

datatype is String

```
String monthNames [] = {"Jan","Feb","Mar","Apr","May",
    "Jun",Jul","Aug","Sep","Oct","Nov","Dec"};
```

The Java array appears as:

Jan	Feb	Mar	Apr	May	Jun	Jul	Aug	Sep	Oct	Nov	Dec
0	1	2	3	4	5	6	7	8	9	10	11

These Java array elements are numbered 0 through 11

NOTES

1. Remember that Java arrays are objects.
2. The array object has a public variable named `length`, which contains the number of elements in the array.
3. We can access this variable using the expression: `arrayname.length`. Notice that the array length is the *number of elements*, and not the number of bytes.

We have written a short Java program to illustrate the declaration and access of one-dimensional arrays. This program, named `OneDimArrayDemo.java`, creates the `numberOfLoans` array, the `monthNames` array, then lists the number of loans by month for the year. The listing for `OneDimArrayDemo.java` is shown in Listing 8.1.

Listing 8.1: `OneDimArrayDemo.java`

```
1. public class OneDimArrayDemo
2. {
3.    public static void main (String args[])
4.    {
5.       // declare loan array & month name array
```

```
6.      int numberOfLoans [] = {39,44,45,65,72,93,14,55,
        67,27,46,82};
7.      String monthNames [] {"Jan","Feb","Mar","Apr",
        "May","Jun","Jul","Aug","Sep","Oct","Nov",
        "Dec"};
8.      int monthNumber; // monthNumber is the index
9.      // print month name & number of loans for the
        // year
10.     monthNumber=0; // index starts at 0 for January
11.     System.out.println ("Loans Month");
12.     while (monthNumber < 12)
        // loop 12 times for 12 months
13.     {
14.        System.out.println (numberOfLoans
           [monthNumber] + " " + monthNames
           [monthNumber]);
15.        monthNumber=monthNumber + 1;
16.     }// end of loop
17.   }// end of main method
18. }// end of OneDimArrayDemo.java
```

This program has only one method—**main()**. This method, instead of being called by another program executes when the program is loaded. The following describes how the program works.

1. Line 6 declares and populates the numberOfLoans array and line 7 the monthNames array.
2. Line 8 declares the index named monthNumber, and line 10 initializes it to zero.
3. Note we could have chosen to declare and initialize it in a single statement: int monthNumber = 0;
4. Line 11 prints a heading for the output.
5. Lines 12 through 16 define the loop that prints the contents of the two arrays. Note the loop is executed 12 times. The first time it is executed, the index contains 0, the second time 1, the third time 2, etc.
6. Within the loop, line 14 prints an element from numberOfLoans and the corresponding element from monthNames. The specific element is determined by the contents of the index, monthNumber.

The output for `OneDimArrayDemo.java` is shown below.

```
Loans Month
39 Jan
44 Feb
45 Mar
65 Apr
72 May
93 Jun
14 Jul
55 Aug
67 Sep
27 Oct
46 Nov
82 Dec
```

DECLARING TWO-DIMENSIONAL ARRAYS

A *two-dimensional* array consists of both rows and columns. To illustrate, let's assume the Community National Bank makes three different types of loans: auto loans, boat loans, and home loans. Also, let's assume that CNB wishes to track the number of loans by type for each month. In other words, they want to know the number of auto, boat, and home loans that were made each month. We can use a two-dimensional array consisting of 3 rows and 12 columns. We assign row 1 to auto loans, row 2 to boat loans, and row 3 to home loans. As before, each column represents a month. Our new array with 3 rows and 12 columns will appear as:

	Jan	Feb	Mar	Apr	May	Jun	Jul	Aug	Sep	Oct	Nov	Dec
Auto Loans												
Boat Loans												
Home Loans												

In COBOL we define this table as:

```
01 LOAN-TABLE.          ──── 3 rows
   05 OCCURS 3 TIMES.                              ──── 12 columns
      10 NUMBER-OF-LOANS PIC 9(3) OCCURS 12 TIMES.
```

We then use two subscripts, one for row number and one for column number, to access a particular element in the array. To display the number of home loans in May (row 3, column 5) we would write:

```
          row 3 ───────          ─── column 5
DISPLAY NUMBER-OF-LOANS (3,  5).
```

This statement will display the number of home loans made by CNB during May.

Declaring two-dimensional arrays in Java is easy—we simply write:

```
int numberOfLoans [][];
                  ─────── two brackets are used for
                          a two-dimensional array
```

Remember that this format does not completely declare the array. We must also write:

```
          3 rows ───────          ─── 12 columns
numberOfLoans = new int [3] [12];
```

to tell the compiler the number of rows and columns we want to have. Similar to the declaration of one-dimensional arrays, we can do all of this in a single statement:

```
int numberOfLoans [] [] = new int [3] [12];
```

To display the number of home loans in May we would write the Java statement:

```
System.out.println (numberOfLoans [2] [4]);
                                  ───       │
              unlike COBOL, each Java      remember—Java begins with
              index is enclosed in a       row 0 and column 0. [2] [4]
              separate bracket             refers to row 3 column 5
```

NOTES

1. Technically, Java does not have two-dimensional arrays that are like COBOL's two-level tables.
2. Remember that a Java array is really an object.

3. A two-dimensional array is an array of arrays.

4. For our purposes here, we pretend we are simply working with two-dimensional arrays.

POPULATING TWO-DIMENSIONAL ARRAYS

As before, we can populate a two-dimensional COBOL array either in the data division using value clauses or use procedural statements in the procedure division.

```
01 LOAN-TABLE-VALUES.
   05 PIC X(36) VALUE
      '012023020021015012005009040020012026'.
   05 PIC X(36) VALUE
      '013010015025035041002016011001019031'.
   05 PIC X(36) VALUE
      '014011010019022040007030016006015025'.
01 LOAN-TABLE REDEFINES LOAN-TABLE-VALUES.
   05 OCCURS 3 TIMES.
10 NUMBER-OF-LOANS PIC 9(3) OCCURS 12 TIMES.
```

The Java code to declare the two-dimensional array for number of loans is:

number of elements
not specified

```
int numberOfLoans [] [] =
{
   {12,23,20,21,15,12,5,9,40,20,12,26}, // auto loans
   {13,10,15,25,35,41,2,16,11,1,19,31}, // boat loans
   {14,11,10,19,22,40,7,30,16,6,15,25}  // home loans
};
```

braces surround values

don't forget the semicolon

values for each row are enclosed in braces & separated by commas

The populated table appears as:

	Jan	Feb	Mar	Apr	May	Jun	Jul	Aug	Sep	Oct	Nov	Dec
Auto Loans	12	23	20	21	15	12	5	9	40	20	12	26
Boat Loans	13	10	15	25	35	41	2	16	11	1	19	31
Home Loans	14	11	10	19	22	40	7	30	16	6	15	25

We have written another small Java program here named TwoDimArray-Demo.java, in Listing 8.2, to illustrate the declaration, population, and access of two-dimensional arrays.

Listing 8.2: `TwoDimArrayDemo.java`

```
1. public class TwoDimArrayDemo
2. {
3.    public static void main (String args[])
4.    {
5.       int numberOfLoans [] [] =
6.       {
7.          {12,23,20,21,15,12,5,9,40,20,12,26},
             // auto loans in row 1
8.          {13,10,15,25,35,41,2,16,11,1,19,31},
             // boat loans in row 2
9.          {14,11,10,19,22,40,7,30,16,6,15,25}
             // home loans in row 3
10.      };
11.      String monthNames [] = {"Jan","Feb","Mar","Apr",
            "May","Jun","Jul","Aug","Sep","Oct","Nov",
            "Dec"};
12.      int typeOfLoan;// row index
13.      int monthNumber;// column index
14.      int numberOfLoansThisMonth;
15.      // print number of boat loans - row 2
16.      monthNumber=0;
17.      System.out.println ("CNB Boat Loans");
18.      System.out.println ("Month Number");
19.      while (monthNumber < 12)// loop 12 times
20.      {
21.         System.out.println (monthNames [monthNumber] +
               " " +
22.         numberOfLoans [1] [monthNumber]);
               // row index remains 1
23.         monthNumber = monthNumber + 1;
24.      }// end of loop to print boat loans
25.      // print the sum of each column (total loans for
            // each month)
```

```
26.      monthNumber = 0;
27.      System.out.println ("CNB Total Loans");
28.      System.out.println ("Month Number");
29.      while (monthNumber < 12)
         // loop 12 times for 12 months
30.      {
31.        numberOfLoansThisMonth = 0;
32.        typeOfLoan = 0;
33.        while (typeOfLoan < 3)
           // loop 3 times to sum this column
34.        {
35.          numberOfLoansThisMonth = numberOfLoans
               ThisMonth + numberOfLoans [typeOfLoan]
               [monthNumber];
36.          typeOfLoan = typeOfLoan + 1;
37.        } // end of row loop
38.        System.out.println (monthNames [monthNumber] +
             " " + numberOfLoansThisMonth);
39.        monthNumber = monthNumber + 1;
40.      }// end of month loop
41.    }// end of main method
42. }// end of TwoDimArrayDemo.java
```

Similar to OneDimArrayDemo.java, TwoDimArrayDemo.java has one **main()** method that is executed when the program is loaded. The following describes how the program works.

1. Lines 5–10 declare and populate the two-dimensional array number-OfLoans.
2. Line 11 populates the monthNames array.
3. Lines 12 and 13 declare the row index (typeOfLoan) and column index (monthNumber).
4. Line 14 declares the loan counter numberOfLoansThisMonth.
5. Lines 15 through 24 print the number of boat loans (row 2) for each month:
   - Line 16 initializes the column index to 0.
   - Lines 17 and 18 display a report heading.
   - Lines 19 through 24 outline a loop that executes 12 times.
     - Line 21 prints the month name and the number of boat loans for the month indicated by the index monthNumber.

- Line 22 increments the column index monthNumber. Note: the index for the row is held constant at 1 (i.e., the second row).
6. Lines 25 through 40 sum and print the total number of loans for each of the 12 months:
   - Line 26 reinitializes the column index monthNumber.
   - Lines 27 and 28 display the report heading.
   - Lines 29 through 40 outline a loop that executes 12 times:
     - Line 31 initializes the counter numberOfLoansThisMonth and line 32 initializes the row index typeOfLoan.
     - Lines 33 through 36 outline a loop that executes 3 times for each month (column).
       - Line 35 sums the numberOfLoansThisMonth.
       - Line 36 increments the row index typeOfLoan.
     - Line 38 prints the month name and numberOfLoansThisMonth.
     - Line 39 increments the column index monthNumber.

Following is the output from TwoDimArrayDemo.java:

```
CNB Boat Loans
Month Number
Jan 13
Feb 10
Mar 15
Apr 25
May 35
Jun 41
Jul 2
Aug 16
Sep 11
Oct 1
Nov 19
Dec 31
CNB Total Loans
Month Number
Jan 39
Feb 44
Mar 45
Apr 65
May 72
```

```
Jun 93
Jul 14
Aug 55
Sep 67
Oct 27
Nov 46
Dec 82
```

A great exercise for you to do at this point is to rewrite one (or more) of the loops in TwoDimArrayDemo.java using the for statement.

PASSING ARRAYS AS ARGUMENTS

We can pass an entire array to a method by simply writing the array name as an argument in the statement calling the method. Or, if we wish, we can pass a single element by specifying the element as an argument. In fact, in TwoDimArrayDemo.java above, we pass an array element when we execute the statement:

println() is
a method

we pass an element of monthNames
to the println() method

```
System.out.println (monthNames [monthNumber] + " " +
    numberOfLoansThisMonth);
```

NOTES

1. When we pass arguments to a method, the method gets a *copy* of the argument.
2. If we pass an object to a method, the method gets a copy of the object reference variable, the pointer to the object. The method has direct access to the object through this reference variable.
3. Java arrays are objects, which means that when we pass an array to a method the method gets a copy of the reference variable and therefore has direct access to the original array.
4. Passing a reference variable is called *passing by reference* because we pass a *reference to the data* instead of a *copy of the data*.

There are two programs at the end of the next section that demonstrate passing arrays to methods.

SEARCHING ARRAYS

In Java, just like in COBOL, we sometimes need to find a specific value in an array. In COBOL we call this searching process a *table look up*. COBOL also has the SEARCH verb that sometimes simplifies a table look up. Java unfortunately has no such facility and we must write the search the old-fashioned way.

The array search logic is essentially the same regardless of the language being used. We look at each of the values in the array until we either find the value we are seeking or get to the end of the array. Specifically, we initialize an index to the beginning of the array, then loop until we find the desired value or reach the end of the array.

To illustrate an array search, we have a 5 element array containing zip codes.

30309 40410 41515 65757 72701

The COBOL code to define this array is:

```
01 ZIP-CODE-VALUES.
   05 PIC X(25) VALUE '3030940410415156575772701'.
01 ZIP-CODE-TABLE REDEFINES ZIP-CODE-VALUES.
   05 ZIP-CODE PIC X(5) OCCURS 5 TIMES.
```

To do the table look up, we will define a program switch (FOUND-IT-SWITCH) to tell us if we find the value, and we will need a subscript (SUB). Let's assume ZIP-ARGUMENT contains the zip code we are seeking.

```
01 ZIP-ARGUMENT        PIC X(5).
01 FOUND-IT-SWITCH     PIC X(3).
   88 FOUND-IT      VALUE 'YES'.
01 SUB                 PIC 9(1).
```

Now, let's write the table lookup in COBOL using an in-line PERFORM-VARYING.

```
MOVE 'NO' TO FOUND-IT-SWITCH
PERFORM VARYING SUB FROM 1 BY 1 UNTIL SUB > 5 OR
  FOUND-IT
    IF ZIP-ARGUMENT=ZIP-CODE (SUB) THEN
      MOVE 'YES' TO FOUND-IT-SWITCH
END-IF
END-PERFORM
IF FOUND-IT THEN
  DISPLAY 'We found it!"
ELSE
  DISPLAY 'We did NOT find it!"
END-IF.
```

Next, we are going to write two little programs to illustrate an array search using Java. This example also demonstrates how to pass an array as an argument to a method.

The first program, FindZipCode.java in Listing 8.3, has one method named **findZip()**. This method receives two parameters from the calling program: zipToFind is a variable that contains the zip code we are searching for and zipCode is an array containing an unknown number of zip codes. The method returns the boolean variable foundIt to inform the calling program whether or not a matching zip code was found.

findZip() is called a *static* method. A *static* method is one that is not associated with a particular object. Instead, it provides a service for the class as a whole. Sometimes we refer to a static method as a *class* method as opposed to an *instance* method. Instance methods provide a service for an object; class methods provide a service for a class. We wrote FindZipCode.java to find zip codes, and therefore, an object of this class is meaningless in this context.

Listing 8.3: FindZipCode.java

```
1.   public class FindZipCode
2.   {
```

static indicates this
is a class method

the first parameter is an integer
variable named `zipToFind`

```
3.   public static boolean findZip (int zipToFind, int
     [] zipCode)
```

the second parameter is an
integer array named `zipCode`

this method returns a
boolean value

```
4.   {
5.        int index = 0;
6.        boolean foundIt = false;
```

`zipCode.length` is the array size

`&&` means "and." `!` means "not"

```
7.      while (index < zipCode.length && !foundIt)
8.      // keep looping until array ends or zipCode
        // found
9.      {
```

`==` means "equal to"

```
10.     if (zipToFind == zipCode [index])
        // is there a match?
11.         foundIt = true;
            // set switch to true if match
12.         else
13.           index++;
            // increase index by 1 if no match
14.     } // end of loop
15.     return foundIt;
16.   } // end of findZip method
17. } // end of FindZipCode.java
```

The second program, `ZipCodeProcessor.java` in Listing 8.4, calls the
findZip() method in `FindZipCode.java`.

Listing 8.4: `ZipCodeProcessor.java`

```
1. public class ZipCodeProcessor
2. {
3.   public static void main(String args[])
```

```
 4.    {
 5.       // declare & populate the array
 6.       int zipCode [] = {30309,40410,41515,65757,72701};
 7.       int zipArgument;
 8.       boolean foundIt;
 9.       zipArgument = 65757;// we should find this value
10.       // call findZip method & pass zipArgument and
          // zipCode array
```

findZip() is a class method, therefore we use the class name instead of an object name in the call

```
11.       foundIt = FindZipCode.findZip (zipArgument,
            zipCode);
12.       if (foundIt)
13.         System.out.println ("We found " +
              zipArgument);
14.       else
15.         System.out.println ("We did NOT find " +
              zipArgument);
16.       // call findZip method again with a different
          // argument
17.       zipArgument = 12345;// we should NOT find this
            value
18.       foundIt = FindZipCode.findZip (zipArgument,
            zipCode);
19.       if (foundIt)
20.         System.out.println ("We found " +
              zipArgument);
21.       else
22.         System.out.println ("We did NOT find " +
              zipArgument);
23.    }// end of main method
24. }// end of ZipCodeProcessor.java
```

Following is a description of how ZipCodeProcessor.java (Listing 8.4) and FindZipCode.java (Listing 8.3) work together.

In ZipCodeProcessor.java (Listing 8.4):

1. Line 6 declares and populates the array zipCode.
2. Line 7 declares the zipArgument and line 8 the boolean variable foundIt.

3. Line 9 stores the zip code value `65757` into `zipArgument`.
4. Line 11 calls **findZip()** in `FindZipCode.java`, passing `zipArgument` containing `65757` and the array named `zipCode` containing `30309`, `40410`, `41515`, `65757`, `72701`

In `FindZipCode.java` (Listing 8.3):

5. Lines 5 and 6 initialize index to 0 and `foundIt` to false.
6. Lines 7 through 12 outline the search loop. The statements inside the loop are executed until we find the zip code or reach the end of the table. Note we use the public variable `length` contained in the array `zipCode` to determine the array size. This means **findZip()** can search an array of any size.
7. Line 9 compares the `zipArgument` to the contents of the array element referenced by `index`. The first time through the loop index contains 0 (pointing to element 1), the second time it contains 1, and so forth. If the values are a match, `foundIt` is set to `true` and the loop terminates.
8. Line 11 increments `index`.
9. Line 13 returns `foundIt` to the calling program, `ZipCodeProcessor.java`.

Back in `ZipCodeProcessor.java` (Listing 8.4):

10. Lines 12 through 15 print the results of the search.
11. Line 16 again calls **findZip()** using a different zip code value.

Output from `ZipCodeProcessor.java`:

```
We found 65757
We did NOT find 12345
```

SUMMARY OF KEY POINTS IN CHAPTER 8

1. COBOL programmers use different array terminology than do Java programmers. Instead of saying "single-level table" and "subscript," Java programmers say "one-dimensional array" and "index."
2. We can declare an array without specifying the number of elements:
`int numberOfLoans [];`

3. We can declare and populate a Java array with one statement:
   ```
   int numberOfLoans
      [] = {39,44,45,65,72,93,14,55,67,27,46,82};
   ```
4. Java array elements begin with index value 0, not 1.
5. Java uses brackets [] instead of parentheses () when referencing an occurrence (element) within an array.
6. Java uses two sets of brackets [] [] for two-dimensional arrays.
7. We can create a Java array of any data type including <u>String</u>.
8. When working with two-dimensional arrays, Java row and column index values begin with 0, not 1.
9. We can pass an array element to a method by simply specifying the element.
10. A Java array is really an object. For the programmer this raises two important issues. First, passing an array to a method makes the *original* array values available to the method. Second, we can access the public array instance variable `arrayname.length` to determine the number of elements in the array. Note this variable contains the number of elements in the array, not the number of bytes.
11. The search logic in Java is similar to the COBOL table look up logic, only the syntax is different.

CHAPTER 9

Data Access

OBJECTIVES

In this chapter you will study:

- Object persistence;
- Sequential file access;
- SQL database access;
- Object serialization; and
- Network access.

This chapter introduces you to Java data access techniques using classes supplied in three packages: `java.io`, `java.sql`, and `java.net`. You are undoubtedly familiar with reading and writing files using COBOL. Java, however, takes a somewhat different approach, and therefore you will not find the clear parallels between COBOL and Java in this chapter that you have seen in the previous chapters.

Here we develop programs to demonstrate sequential file input-output (I-O) and database access. In addition we demonstrate a technique called *object serialization* used by Java to store intact objects in files for later retrieval. Although a demonstration of network access is beyond the scope of this book, we will present an overview.

The chapter begins with a brief description of the I-O classes contained in the `java.io` package and their hierarchy. Then, a relatively simple sequential file I-O demonstration is presented. Next we repeat the example using a relational database. Object persistence is then discussed and illustrated using Java's Object Serialization classes. The chapter concludes with a discussion of network access using classes in the `java.net` package.

This chapter assumes you understand the following:

Java:
  OO concepts (Chapter 2)
  Java program structure (Chapter 3)
  Defining data (Chapter 4)
  Decision making (Chapter 6)
  Looping (Chapter 7)
  Arrays (Chapter 8)

JAVA'S I-O CLASS LIBRARY (`java.io`)

The basic purpose of the classes contained in the `java.io` package is to provide tools to input and output data. This data can be going to any output device or coming from any input device. These classes take care of reading, writing, converting, and parsing data for our programs.

Java uses the term *data stream* to refer to any input or output data. A Java stream is simply a flow of bytes of data, either into or out of a program. A program reads data from an *input stream* and writes data to an *output stream*, regardless of the data source or destination. This abstraction keeps our code device independent—we don't worry about the particular I-O device we are using. We simply refer to the appropriate stream.

Java actually has two kinds of streams: *byte streams* store data in Unicode format (2 bytes per character), and *character stream* data is stored in the native format of the system where the data is being used. Character streams are automatically converted back to Unicode when read by our program.

Using the stream concept, we can have data I-O without being particularly concerned about the physical device to which the data is flowing. Remember that Java programs are designed to be highly portable. We want to avoid having our program code being device dependent.

```
File (objects represent physical files)
InputStream (superclass for byte input streams)
        FileInputStream (reads an input stream)
        ObjectInputStream (reads objects from a file)
OutputStream (superclass for byte output streams)
        FileOutputStream (writes an output stream)
        ObjectOutputStream (writes objects to a file)
                RandomAccessFile (provides random file access)
Reader (superclass for character input streams)
        InputStreamReader
        FileReader
StreamTokenizer (parses text files into data items (tokens))
Writer (superclass for character output streams)
        PrintWriter
```

FIGURE **9.1. Partial `java.io` class hierarchy.**

A partial list of the `java.io` class hierarchy is shown in Figure 9.1.

OBJECT PERSISTENCE

Until now we have ignored the issue of storing objects for later retrieval. We created objects and worked with them, but conveniently avoided the problem of keeping them for future use. For example, we created <u>Customer</u> and <u>Account</u> objects, but these disappeared when our programs stopped running. In the real world, we obviously need objects to be stored for subsequent processing.

A *persistent* object is one with a life longer than the execution of the program that creates it. In contrast, a *transient* object lives only as long as the program that created it is executing. In most applications, we need persistent objects, although until now we have worked only with transient objects.

There are numerous options for storing objects, or at least the data contained in the objects. For example, we can write the data to a sequential file, store it in a relational database, or use a Java technique called *object serialization* to store complete, intact objects. In the following sections we demonstrate all three approaches.

SEQUENTIAL FILE I-O

If we wish to store the Customer data in a COBOL sequential file we first define the file:

```
FD CUSTOMER-FILE.
01 CUSTOMER-RECORD.
05 CUSTOMER-NAME    PIC X(25).
05 SS-NO            PIC X(9).
05 ADDRESS          PIC X(35).
05 PHONE-NUMBER     PIC X(10).
```

Then write code to create the file

```
OPEN OUTPUT CUSTOMER-FILE
 .
 .
WRITE CUSTOMER-RECORD
 .
 .
CLOSE CUSTOMER-FILE
```

To read the data, we would write:

```
OPEN INPUT CUSTOMER-FILE
 .
 .
READ CUSTOMER-FILE
AT END MOVE "YES" TO EOF-SW
END-READ
 .
 .
CLOSE CUSTOMER-FILE
```

As in COBOL, we can store Java data in a sequential file. The following example illustrates one approach by writing customer data to a text file named `Customer.txt`, then reading the values back in and displaying them.

The steps to write to a text file are:

1. Create a <u>File</u> object containing the filespec for our file:

```
File aFile = new File ("filespec");
```

Class name   Object name;   provided by developer
                    provided by developer

2. Create a FileOutputStream object using the File object created in Step 1:

```
FileOutputStream fo = new FileOutputStream (aFile);
```

Class name   Object name;   From step 1
                provided by developer

3. Create a PrintStream object using the FileOutputStream object created in Step 2:

```
PrintStream ps = new PrintStream(fo);
```

Class name   Object name;   From step 2
                    provided by developer

4. Call the **println()** method of the PrintStream class to write a data item. The argument is the variable name of the data item we wish to write:

```
ps.println(variable_name);
```

The steps to read data from a text file are similar:

1. Create a File object containing the filespec for our file:

```
File aFile = new File ("filespec");
```

2. Create a FileInputStream object using the File object created in Step 1:

```
FileInputStream fi = new FileInputStream (aFile);
```

3. Create a DataInputStream object using the FileInputStream object created in Step 2:

```
DataInputStream i = new DataInputStream(fi);
```

4. Call the **readLine()** method of the DataInputStream class:

```
variable_name = i.readline();
```

Here we illustrate sequential file I-O by writing customer data to a text file, and then reading the values back in and displaying them.

To write the program named `SequentialFileDemo.java`, we first import the classes from the `java.io` package:

```
import java.io.*;
```

Then we create a File object, which identifies the file we will use:

```
// create a File object for Customer.txt
File customerFile = new File
  ("C:/Customers/Customer.txt");
```

Notice that we use the forward slash "/" instead of the backward slash "\."
Java uses the backward slash as an *escape* character, which is used to indicate
special characters such as new line "\n" and backspace "\b." The forward slash
"/" is converted into whatever the system running the program needs. For
example, the program here was written and executed on a Windows machine,
but will work equally well on a UNIX system.

Next we create and populate the attributes for <u>Customer</u>:

```
// data for the output file
String name = "Jed Muzzy";
String ssNo = "499444471";
String address = "P.O. Box 1881, Great Falls, MT 59601";
String phoneNumber = "None";
```

Now, write the attribute values to customerFile. Note that we use the try-
catch structure because **println()** can throw an IOException.

```
try
{
   FileOutputStream fo = new FileOutputStream
     (customerFile);
   PrintStream ps = new PrintStream(fo);
   ps.println(name);
   ps.println(ssNo);
   ps.println(address);
   ps.println(phoneNumber);
}
catch (Exception event)
{
   System.out.println ("I/O error during write to
     CustomerFile");
}
```

Then we read the data back and display it. We again use try-catch because
readLine() can also throw an IOException.

```
// now read it back
try
{
   FileInputStream fi = new FileInputStream
     (customerFile);
```

```
        DataInputStream i = new DataInputStream(fi);
        name = i.readLine();
        ssNo = i.readLine();
        address = i.readLine();
        phoneNumber = i.readLine();
        System.out.println ("Name: " + name);
        System.out.println ("SS No: " + ssNo);
        System.out.println ("Address: " + address);
        System.out.println ("Phone: " + phoneNumber);
    }
    catch (Exception event)
        {
            System.out.println ("I/O error during read from
              CustomerFile");
        }
```

The program output is:

```
Name: Jed Muzzy
SS No: 499444471
Address: P.O. Box 1881, Great Falls, MT 59601
Phone: None
```

The complete program listing for SequentialFileDemo.java is shown in Listing 9.1.

Listing 9.1: SequentialFileDemo.java

```
import java.io.*;
public class FileDemo
{
    public static void main(String args[])
    {
        // data for the output file
        String name = "Jed Muzzy";
        String ssNo = "499444471";
        String address = "P.O. Box 1881, Great Falls,
          MT 59601";
        String phoneNumber = "None";
```

```java
    // create a text file containing Customer attributes
    File customerFile = new File
      ("C:/Customers/Customer.txt");
    try
    {
      FileOutputStream fo = new FileOutputStream
        (customerFile);
      PrintStream ps = new PrintStream(fo);
      ps.println(name);
      ps.println(ssNo);
      ps.println(address);
      ps.println(phoneNumber);
    }
catch (Exception event)
{
   System.out.println ("I/O error during write to
     CustomerFile");
}
// now, read it back in
try
{
   FileInputStream fi = new FileInputStream
     (customerFile);

   DataInputStream i = new DataInputStream(fi);
   name = i.readLine();
   ssNo = i.readLine();
   address = i.readLine();
   phoneNumber = i.readLine();
   System.out.println ("Name: " + name);
   System.out.println ("SS No: " + ssNo);
   System.out.println ("Address: " + address);
   System.out.println ("Phone: " + phoneNumber);
}
catch (Exception event)
{
   System.out.println ("I/O error during read from
     CustomerFile");}
} // end main
} // end SequentialFileDemo.java
```

Take note of a couple of important points concerning this example. First, the example really does nothing more than write some data to secondary storage, then read it back. To use this storage technique with our Customer class, we would need to write methods to send and retrieve the attribute values being stored. Second, a Customer object is not being stored—only the values of the attributes of a particular Customer object are stored. To use the information, the data would have to be retrieved and inserted into a "blank" Customer object. Using sequential files, as just illustrated, would require the following conceptual steps for proper OO programming:

To store data:

1. Accept input from user (or other sources).
2. Create a Customer object and populate the object with data from input source.
3. Send a message to the class handling data management for Customer requesting storage of the data; the message should contain the attribute values to be stored.

To retrieve data:

1. Create a Customer object.
2. Send a message to the class handling data management for Customer requesting the data; the message should return the attribute values for the object.
3. Populate the blank Customer object with the retrieved values.

DATABASE ACCESS

Today, many organizations use relational databases to store data. A relational database contains data stored in tables consisting of rows and columns. Each column is a field or data item and each row is a record or entity. A table for Customer would have four columns: Name, SSNo., Address, and Phone. The table would have a separate row for each customer. (See Figure 9.2, Customer Database Table.)

We can have multiple tables that are related. For example, at Community National we could have a table for Customer and another for CheckingAccount. These tables would be connected with a relationship

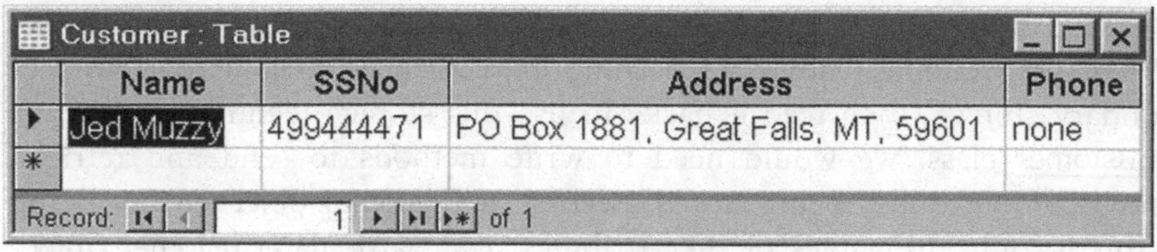

Customer : Table

	Name	SSNo	Address	Phone
▸	Jed Muzzy	499444471	PO Box 1881, Great Falls, MT, 59601	none
*				

Record: 1 of 1

FIGURE 9.2. Customer database table.

(i.e., a common key field). For example, we could add the customer's `SSNo` to the `Account` table, then we could find the owner of an account or all the accounts owned by a particular customer.

Structured Query Language (SQL) is a standardized (ANSI 1986, 1989, 1992, and 1999) database language with widespread acceptance and use. SQL provides a set of English-like statements to access and manipulate data in a relational database. The SQL `Select` statement is used to retrieve data. We simply write the name of the columns we want retrieved. For example, to retrieve all four `Customer` fields, we write:

```
Select Name, SSNo, Address, Phone from Customer
```

We will demonstrate this `Select` in two examples: one with COBOL, the other with Java.

In the following COBOL example (Listing 9.2), the data from a relational database table (as shown in Figure 9.2) is extracted and displayed. Basically, SQL is "embedded" in traditional COBOL code using syntax specific to database operations. Note: the syntax may vary slightly due to the type of database and compiler used.

Listing 9.2: COBOL SQL Example

```
Identification Division.
...
Data Division.
Working-Storage Section.
Detail-line
05 DL-Name PIC X(20).
05 DL-SSN PIC X(9).
05 DL-Address PIC X(40).
05 DL-Phone PIC X(13).
```

```
      *

      EXEC SQL BEGIN DECLARE SECTION END-EXEC.
* This begins the section which will hold the variables
* from the table (we'll call them host variables)
   01 HV-Name PIC X(20).
   01 HV-SSN PIC X(9).
  01 HV-Address PIC X(40).
  01 HV-Phone PIC X(13).

  *

  EXEC SQL END DECLARE SECTION END-EXEC.
* End of the variable section
  *

  EXEC SQL INCLUDE SQLCA END-EXEC.
  PROCEDURE DIVISION.
  MAIN-CONTROL.

  *

  EXEC SQL DECLARE C CURSOR FOR
  SELECT NAME, SSN, ADDRESS, PHONE FROM CUSTOMER
  END-EXEC.
* A 'cursor' is used to hold a set of data from the
* the table; holds multiple rows

  *

* Open the cursor
   EXEC SQL OPEN C END-EXEC.
* Now, read the data from the cursor and display it

  *

PERFORM UNTIL SQLCODE NOT = 0
EXEC SQL FETCH C
   INTO :HV-NAME, :HV-SSN, :HV-ADDRESS, :HV-PHONE
END-EXEC
MOVE HV-NAME TO DL-NAME
MOVE HV-SSN TO DL-SSN
MOVE HV-ADDRESS TO DL-ADDRESS
```

```
MOVE HV-PHONE TO DL-PHONE
DISPLAY DETAIL-LINE
END-PERFORM.

*


EXEC SQL CLOSE C END-EXEC.
STOP RUN.
```

Fortunately, Java provides facilities for easy database access. The Java database connectivity (JDBC) class program library is contained in the `java.sql` package. This package provides classes and methods that enable us to write programs to access relational databases using SQL. JDBC is both platform and database independent and is intended to provide a seamless interface to any SQL relational database, including both remote and local databases. (For additional JDBC information, go to http://java.sun.com/products/jdbc.)

We use four `java.sql` classes to access relational databases:

1. **DriverManager** – creates and maintains database connections.
2. **Connection** – represents each database connection.
3. **Statement** – executes SQL statements.
4. **ResultSet** – contains data that is retrieved from the database.

There is also an exception class named **SQLException** used to contain error messages and vendor-specific codes resulting from the execution of SQL statements. A single SQL statement can generate multiple **SQLException** objects and we should access them all.

To demonstrate Java database access, we first create a simple database containing one table: `Customer`. This example uses Microsoft Access, but it could be any SQL relational database. First we create a table that contains our four columns: `Name`, `SSNo`, `Address`, and `Phone`. Here, the table is populated with our customer, Jed Muzzy, as shown in Figure 9.2.

Let's write a small Java program named `DataBaseDemo.java` to retrieve customer data using the JDBC SQL interface tools. First, we tell the Java compiler to import the SQL package:

```
import java.sql.*;
```

Then we declare variables to contain the retrieved data:

```
// declare variables for the data
String name, ssNo, address, phoneNumber;
```

JDBC uses a Uniform Resource Locator (URL) to identify databases. We define a String variable to contain the URL database identification:

```
// declare url for the database
String url = "jdbc:odbc:Customers";
// The DB name is "Customers"
```

The use of odbc in the above string is based on the type of database we are using for this particular example, MS-Access. ODBC (Open Database Connectivity) is a Microsoft-sponsored standard for database connectivity. Other database types may require a different set of drivers.

We also define a String variable to contain the SQL Select statement that we will execute to retrieve the customer data:

```
// define the SQL query statement
String sqlQuery = "SELECT Name, SSNo, Address, Phone
  FROM Customer";
```

The statements to establish a database connection and retrieve data can throw an exception. Therefore, we use the try-catch structure for this code. Our database example is running on a MS Windows system, and we first load the appropriate driver using the class method **forName()**.

```
try
{ // load the jdbc - odbc bridge driver for MS-Windows
    Class.forName("sun.jdbc.odbc.JdbcOdbcDriver");
```

We next create a Connection object using the **getConection()** method in the <u>DriverManager</u> class. "JavaDemo" is the ID and "JavaIsFun" is the password required to access the database.

```
// create Connection object
Connection aConnection =
DriverManager.getConnection(url, "JavaDemo",
  "JavaIsFun");
```

Then we call the connection method **createStatement()** to create a <u>Statement</u> object to execute the SQL code:

```
// create Statement object
Statement aStatement = aConnection.createStatement();
```

Finally, we execute the SQL statement contained in `sqlQuery` by calling **executeQuery()**. The data returned is contained in the <u>ResultSet</u> object named **rs**.

```
// execute the SQL query statement
ResultSet rs = aStatement.executeQuery(sqlQuery);
```

Following the successful execution of the SQL `Select` statement, the <u>ResultSet</u> object, **rs**, contains the data arranged in rows, one row per customer. The method **next()** moves a logical pointer to the next row of data and returns a `boolean` value `true` or `false` indicating if there is more data or not.

```
// get first row of data
boolean more = rs.next();
```

Once we have a pointer to a row of data, we then call the <u>ResultSet</u> method **getString()** to retrieve data from a specific column (here all of our data are strings, but there are additional methods for other data types such as **getFloat()**, **getInt()**, and so on).

Although in this example, we have only one row of data (one customer) we have written a loop that will process multiple rows. A good exercise here is to create your own `Customer` database with several customers, then use `DataBaseDemo.java` to retrieve and list all of them for you.

```
while (more) // loop while there are rows of data
{
    // extract the data & display
    name = rs.getString(1);
    ssNo = rs.getString(2);
    address = rs.getString(3);
    phoneNumber = rs.getString(4);
    System.out.println("Name: " + name);
    System.out.println("SS No: " + ssNo);
    System.out.println("Address: " + address);
    System.out.println("Phone: " + phoneNumber);

    // get next row
    more = rs.next();
} // end while loop
```

We then close the connection and end the `try` block:

```
    rs.close();           // close everything
    aStatement.close();
    aConnection.close();
} // end try
```

The first `catch` block used in this example traps the `ClassNotFoundException`, which will be thrown if the appropriate driver is not loaded.

```
catch (ClassNotFoundException e)
{
    System.out.println("Exception caught "+ e);
}
```

The second `catch` block traps errors encountered during the SQL execution. As we indicated above, a single SQL statement can result in multiple exceptions being thrown. Here we write a loop to identify all of those that may be thrown.

```
catch (SQLException e)
{
    while (e != null) // we can have multiple exceptions
    {
        System.out.println("SQLException caught "+ e);
        e = e.getNextException();
    } // end while loop
} // end catch
```

The program output is the same as before:

```
Name: Jed Muzzy
SS No: 499444471
Address: P.O. Box 1881, Great Falls, MT 59601
Phone: None
```

The complete program is provided in Listing 9.3.

Listing 9.3: `DatabaseDemo.java`

```java
// Demonstrate SQL Database Access
// DataBaseDemo.java
import java.sql.*;
public class DataBaseDemo
{
   public static void main(String args[])
   {
      // declare variables for the data
      String name, ssNo, address, phoneNumber;
      // declare url for the database
      String url = "jdbc:odbc:Customers";
      // The dB name is "Customers"
      // define the SQL query statement
      String sqlQuery = "SELECT Name, SSNo, Address,
       Phone FROM Customer";
      try
      { // load the jdbc - odbc bridge driver for
       // Windows-95
         Class.forName("sun.jdbc.odbc.JdbcOdbcDriver");
         // create Connection object
         // "JavaDemo" is ID & "JavaIsFun" is password
         Connection aConnection =
           DriverManager.getConnection(url, "JavaDemo",
             JavaIsFun");
         // create Statement object
         Statement aStatement =
          aConnection.createStatement();
         // execute the SQL query statement
         ResultSet rs = aStatement.executeQuery(sqlQuery);

         // get first row
         boolean more = rs.next();
         while (more) // loop while there are rows of data
         { // extract the data & display
            name = rs.getString(1);
            ssNo = rs.getString(2);
            address = rs.getString(3);
```

```
            phoneNumber = rs.getString(4);
            System.out.println("Name: " + name);
            System.out.println("SS No: " + ssNo);
            System.out.println("Address: " + address);
            System.out.println("Phone: " + phoneNumber);
            // get next row
            more = rs.next();
         } // end while loop
         rs.close();    // close everything
         aStatement.close();
         aConnection.close();
      } // end try
      catch (ClassNotFoundException e)
      {
         System.out.println("Exception caught "+ e);
      }
      catch (SQLException e)
      {
         while (e != null) // we can have multiple
                           // exceptions
         {
           System.out.println("SQLException caught "+ e);
           e = e.getNextException();
         } // end while loop
      } // end catch
   } // end main
 } // end DataBaseDemo.java
```

OBJECT SERIALIZATION

In the previous two sections we used sequential files and relational databases
to accomplish object persistence. In reality, however, only the values of the
object's attributes were being stored. The actual object was not stored. In
this section we illustrate a convenient technique called *object serialization* to
store whole objects (not just attributes) for future access. Object serialization
is a Java technique available with JDK used to store objects in a file with all
of their relevant information so that we can retrieve them in the same state
as when they were stored. This means the retrieved objects have all of their

original attribute values, methods, and relationships. We cannot distinguish between a newly created object and one that has been retrieved using object serialization. This is in sharp contrast to storing only the *attribute values* of objects. Object serialization stores complete, intact objects.

The steps to *store* an object are:

1. Create a <u>File</u> object containing the filespec for our file:
   ```
   File aFile = new File ("filespec");
   ```
2. Create a <u>FileOutputStream</u> object using the <u>File</u> object created in Step 1 :
   ```
   FileOutputStream fo = new FileOutputStream
     (aFile);
   ```
   Note: the first two steps are the same as the sequential file process illustrated earlier.
3. Create an <u>ObjectOutputStream</u> object using the <u>FileOutputStream</u> object created in Step 2:
   ```
   ObjectOutputStream o = new ObjectOutputStream(fo);
   ```
   Class name   Object name;   From step 2
                                 provided by developer

4. Call the **writeObject()** method of the <u>ObjectOutputStream</u> class. The arguments are the reference variables for the objects we wish to store:
   ```
   o.writeObject(object_reference_variables);
   ```

The steps to *retrieve* an object are similar:

1. Create a <u>File</u> object containing the filespec for our file:
   ```
   File aFile = new File ("filespec");
   ```
2. Create a <u>FileInputStream</u> object using the <u>File</u> object created in Step 1 :
   ```
   FileInputStream fi = new FileInputStream (aFile);
   ```
   Note: the first two steps are the same as the sequential file process illustrated earlier.
3. Create an <u>ObjectInputStream</u> object using the <u>FileInputStream</u> object created in Step 2:
   ```
   ObjectInputStream i = new ObjectInputStream(fi);
   ```
4. Call the **readObject()** method of the <u>ObjectInputStream</u> object:
   ```
   object_reference_variable = i.readObject();
   ```
   `object_reference_variable` refers to the object being retrieved.

We can store any number of objects using this technique. Also, the objects do not have to be from the same class. For example, we could store both <u>Customer</u> and <u>CheckingAccount</u> objects in the same file.

Here we illustrate object persistence using object serialization by creating a <u>Customer</u> object, writing it to a file, then retrieving it and displaying the attribute values. We use the existing class program `Customer.java` from Chapter 3, but we *implement* the <u>Serializable</u> interface.

```
public class Customer implements java.io.Serializable
```

We then write a new class program, named `ObjectSerialization-Demo.java` to create, store, and retrieve the <u>Customer</u> object. This new program is patterned closely after the previous `CustomerProcessor.java` program. Remember, however, the objects previously created by `Customer-Processor.java` had a very short life; they expired when the program terminated. The objects created in this example are persistent. They reside in a file named `Customer.dat` and are available for retrieval whenever needed.

To write `ObjectSerializationDemo.java`, we first import the classes from the `java.io` package needed for serialization:

```
import java.io.*;
```

Then we create a <u>File</u> object, which identifies the specific file we will use:

```
// create a File object for Customer.dat
File customerFile = new File
  ("C:/Customers/Customer.dat");
```

Next we create a <u>Customer</u> object using a reference variable named aCustomer:

```
// create a Customer object
String name = "Jed Muzzy";
String ssNo = "499444471";
String address = "P.O. Box 1881, Great Falls,
  MT 59601";
String phoneNumber = "None";
Customer aCustomer = new Customer(name, ssNo, address,
  phoneNumber);
```

Now, let's write the object to `customerFile`. Note that we must use the `try-catch` structure because the method **writeObject()** can throw an `IOException`. Java will not compile our program unless we make provision to handle the exception.

```
try
{
    FileOutputStream fo = new FileOutputStream
      (customerFile);
    ObjectOutputStream o = new ObjectOutputStream (fo);

    o.writeObject(aCustomer); // write the object
}
catch (IOException event)
{
    System.out.println ("I/O error during write to
      customerFile");
}
```

Then we read the object back and display the attribute values, but this time we use a different reference variable, aNewCustomer. We again must use `try-catch` because **writeObject()** can also throw an `IOException`.

```
try
{
    FileInputStream fi = new FileInputStream
      (customerFile);

    ObjectInputStream i = new ObjectInputStream (fi);
    // read object
    Customer aNewCustomer = (Customer) i.readObject();
    // then display the attributes from retrieved customer
    object System.out.println ("Name: " +
      NewCustomer.getName());

    System.out.println ("SS No: " +
      aNewCustomer.getSSNo());

    System.out.println ("Address: " +
      NewCustomer.getAddress());
```

```
    System.out.println ("Phone: " +
      NewCustomer.getPhoneNumber());

}
catch (IOException event)
{
    System.out.println ("I/O error during read from
      customerFile");
}
```

The program output is exactly the same as the previous two examples:

```
Name: Jed Muzzy
SS No: 499444471
Address: P.O. Box 1881, Great Falls, MT 59601
Phone: None
```

The complete program for ObjectSerializationDemo.java is shown in Listing 9.4.

Listing 9.4: `ObjectSerializationDemo.java`

```
// Demonstrate Object Persistence using Serialization
//
// ObjectSerializationDemo.java
import java.io.*;
public class ObjectSerializationDemo
{
    public static void main (String args[])
    {
        // create a File object for Customer.dat
        File customerFile = new File
          ("C:/Customers/Customer.dat");
        // create a Customer object
        String name = "Jed Muzzy";
        String ssNo = "499444471";
        String address = "P.O. Box 1881, Great Falls,
          MT 59601";
        String phoneNumber = "None";
```

```java
Customer aCustomer = new Customer(name, ssNo,
  address, phoneNumber);
Customer aNewCustomer;
// and store it in "Customer.dat"
try
{
  FileOutputStream fo = new FileOutputStream
    (customerFile);
  ObjectOutputStream o = new ObjectOutputStream
    (fo);
  o.writeObject(aCustomer); // write the object
}
catch (Exception event)
{
  System.out.println ("I/O error during write to
    CustomerFile");
}
// now read it back
try
{
  FileInputStream fi = new FileInputStream
    (customerFile);
  ObjectInputStream i = new ObjectInputStream (fi);
  // read an object and cast it to type Customer
  // read the object
  aNewCustomer = (Customer) i.readObject();
  // display attributes from retrieved Customer
  // objects
  System.out.println ("Name: " +
    aNewCustomer.getName());
  System.out.println ("SS No: " +
    aNewCustomer.getSSNo());
  System.out.println ("Address: " +
    aNewCustomer.getAddress());
  System.out.println ("Phone:" +
    aNewCustomer.getPhoneNumber());
}
catch (Exception event)
{
```

```
        System.out.println ("I/O error during read
            customerFile");
    }
    } // end main
} // end of ObjectSerializationDemo.java
```

NETWORK ACCESS

Classes in the `java.net` package provide us with a rich set of tools for accessing systems connected to a network, either an intranet or the Internet. Java's network communications are based on the client-server computing model.

Java, like most communications programs, uses the *socket* concept to provide network connections. The Socket class in the `java.net` package is used in network communication. A Socket object is an interface to a communications link between a client and server. Java programs read and write data to an object of the Socket class, but they use an input or output stream to do so.

The server attaches a Socket object to a communications port and waits to receive a client request. The client program uses a Socket object to establish communication with the server program, then reads and writes data through the Socket object using one of the I-O streams previously discussed.

World Wide Web access is also provided by classes in `java.net`. We connect to a URL using a URL object containing the URL access information. We then create a DataInputStream object from the `java.io` package and use the **readLine()** method to input data from the URL.

If we wish to both read and write to the URL, we need to also create a URLConnection object, then create both DataInputStream and DataOutputStream objects to read and write data.

SUMMARY OF KEY POINTS IN CHAPTER 9

1. The `java.io` package contains classes to perform data input and output. A Java *stream* is simply a flow of bytes of data, either into or out of our program. Our program reads data from an *input stream* and writes data to an *output stream* instead of a physical device.
2. Java uses two kinds of streams: *byte streams* store data in Unicode (2 bytes per character) format, and *character stream* data are stored in the native format of the machine being used.

3. A *persistent* object is an object stored in a file that can be retrieved for later processing. A *transient* object is one that exists only while the program is running. When the program terminates, the object is erased from memory.

4. Objects can be stored a variety of common ways, including sequential files and relational databases. However, these traditional data storage methods only store the attributes of the objects. *Object serialization*, a technique provide by Java, allows for true object persistence.

5. Java accesses relational databases using classes in the `java.sql` package.

6. Object serialization is a technique to store objects in a file. We use the ObjectOutputStream class to store the objects and the ObjectInputStream class to retrieve them. Objects stored using this technique appear *exactly the same* when they are retrieved as when they were stored.

7. Classes in the `java.net` package allow us to access systems connected to a network, either an Intranet or the Internet.

CHAPTER 10

Graphical User Interfaces

OBJECTIVES

In this chapter you will study:

- Designing & writing GUI programs;
- Java's Swing GUI components;
- Event-driven programming;
- Creating & displaying windows;
- Adding buttons to windows;
- Using text fields, labels, & panels;
- Adding menus to windows; and
- Writing applets.

This chapter introduces you to writing graphical user interfaces (GUIs) using classes in the `javax.swing` package. The material presented here does not have a direct COBOL counterpart. However, having an overview of the GUI capabilities of Java Swing components is important, especially since it clearly demonstrates the relationships between GUI and Problem Domain classes.

The chapter begins with a brief description of the `javax.swing` package and event-driven programming. Then we illustrate how to display and close a Java window. Next we add push buttons, labels, and text fields to the window

FIGURE 10.1. A completed Community National Bank GUI.

to create a functioning GUI program to input new customer information for the Community National Bank. Then we add drop-down menus to the program. The chapter concludes with the creation of an applet to enter new customer information for the bank.

This chapter assumes you understand the following:

Java:
   OO concepts (Chapter 2)
   Java program structure (Chapter 3)
   Defining data (Chapter 4)
   Arithmetic (Chapter 5)
   Decision making (Chapter 6)
   Looping (Chapter 7)

JAVA'S SWING COMPONENTS

A user interface is what the user sees on the computer screen when interfacing with an application. A graphical user interface (GUI, pronounced "GOO-EE") is the combination of graphical elements (windows, menus, labels, text fields, buttons, etc.) that form the user interface. Nearly all applications use a GUI and users have come to expect them. A well-designed GUI makes the application much easier to use. The appearance and functionality of a GUI is often known as the application's look and feel. An example of a completed GUI for the Community National Bank application is shown in Figure 10.1.

The GUI in Figure 10.1 has a window with a title bar (New Customer), a menu bar (containing File and Help menus), four labels (Name:, SS No.:, Address:, and Phone No.:), four corresponding text fields (all of which contain optional text to guide the user), and two buttons (Accept and Clear). The particular arrangement of these elements is achieved using various kinds of Java layout commands.

A Java GUI consists of components (objects) with which the user interacts via a mouse, keyboard, or other type of input device. Java uses a variety of built-in classes to create GUI components. These classes are part of the `javax.swing` package, so they are called Swing components and have become standard with the release of the Java 2 platform version of 1.2. Swing is a large and complex topic, so only a subset of all the Java GUI components is presented in this chapter.

In earlier versions of Java, GUI's were created using the Abstract Windowing Toolkit (AWT), or `java.awt` package. However, the look and feel of AWT GUIs were platform dependent (e.g., Unix, Windows, or Macintosh). With most Swing components, the look and feel of the GUI becomes platform independent, and the look and feel can even be changed during program execution (if desired). In Java 2, AWT was updated to enable Swing components, which use AWT, to be platform independent.

Figure 10.2 shows the hierarchy of some of the AWT and Swing classes. Note that the Swing class names begin with the letter "J." The <u>Component</u> class inherits attributes and behaviors from the <u>Object</u> class, the <u>Container</u> class inherits from the <u>Component</u> class, and the <u>JComponents</u> class inherits from the <u>Container</u> class. Thus, a <u>JComponent</u> object is a <u>Container</u> object, as well as a <u>Component</u> object and an <u>Object</u> object. Operations common to most GUI components (either Swing or AWT) are found in the <u>Component</u> class. Most Swing components (like labels, text fields, and buttons) are <u>JComponent</u> objects and are added to <u>Container</u> objects, such as a content pane. The <u>LayoutManager</u> class inherits directly from <u>Object</u> and is used to organize components in a GUI. The classes shown in **boldface** are those covered in this chapter.

Before you can write a GUI program, however, you need to understand the basics of event-driven programming and event handling. Although you may have written event-driven programs using other languages, Java's approach is somewhat different. Remember, Java is object-oriented.

EVENT-DRIVEN PROGRAMMING

GUI's are event-driven. Events are generated when the user performs an action, such as clicking a button with a mouse. Other common user actions are moving a mouse pointer, clicking a text field, typing in a text field, and

Object (in Java, everything is an object)

    Component (everything in a GUI is a component)
      Container
        Window
          Frame
            JFrame (our GUI applications *extend* this class)
          JComponent
            JButton (used to trigger an event)
            JLabel (used to display information to the user)
            JPanel (invisible container for other GUI components)
        Panel
          Applet
            JApplet (executes within a browser program)
       TextComponent
        TextField
          JTextField (used to display and enter data)

      MenuComponent
        MenuBar
          JMenuBar (contains one or more menus)
        Menu
          JMenu (contains multiple menu items)
        MenuItem
          JMenuItem (a menu selection that triggers an event)

    LayoutManager (positions GUI components in a frame)
      FlowLayout
      BorderLayout
      GridLayout
      BoxLayout
      GridBagLayout

FIGURE 10.2. A partial AWT and Swing class hierarchy.

selecting an item from a menu. When such a user action occurs, the program creates an event object from either the `java.awt.event` class or the `javax.swing.event` class.

Java incorporates an elaborate event-handling mechanism that consists of three parts: the event source, the event object, and the event listener. The event source is the object (GUI component) with which the user interacts (such as a button). The event object is created when an action occurs—it holds important event information. The event listener is an object that receives the event object when the event source detects an event and uses the event object to respond. These event listeners are objects of a class that implements one or more of the event-listener interfaces from the `java.awt.event` or `javax.swing.event` packages.

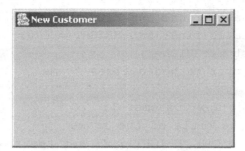

FIGURE **10.3. Frame with no component.**

The programmer must register an event listener with each GUI component that is expected to generate an event (such as a button), and implement event-handling methods containing code to deal with the event. An event-listener object "listens" for events generated by event sources in the GUI. The event handler is a method in an event-listener interface that is called in response to a specific type of event.

JFRAME: DISPLAYING & CLOSING A WINDOW

Listing 10.1 provides a program (`CustomerGUIOne.java`) that produces a simple frame (or window) with no contents. The CustomerGUIOne class has two variables and two methods—a constructor method to define a CustomerGUIOne frame object and a main method to create and display a CustomerGUIOne frame object. Note that the variables WIDTH and HEIGHT are private (available only to this class), static (class-wide information available to all objects of this class), and final (value cannot be changed during program execution). Figure 10.3 displays the result.

Listing 10.1—`CustomerGUIOne.java`

```
// Create a GUI with no contents
import javax.swing.*; // import Swing package
// this class inherits methods from the JFrame class
public class CustomerGUIOne extends JFrame
{
    // static final variables to hold frame dimensions in
    // pixels
```

```
private static final int WIDTH = 275;
private static final int HEIGHT = 170;
public CustomerGUIOne()
// constructor method defines frame
{
   setTitle("New Customer");
   // set the title of the frame
   setSize(WIDTH, HEIGHT); // set the frame size
} // end constructor method
public static void main(String [] args)
//declare main() method
{
   // create the frame object
   JFrame aCustomerGUIOne = new CustomerGUIOne();
   aCustomerGUIOne.show(); // display the frame
} // end main
} // end class
```

The program begins by importing the `javax.swing` package, which is needed since the <u>JFrame</u> class is contained in the `javax.swing` package. Notice that the <u>CustomerGUIOne</u> class declaration uses the code `extends JFrame` in order for this class to inherit the public methods of the <u>JFrame</u> class (such as **setTitle()**, **setSize()**, and **show()**). Next, the class declares and initializes two static (and final) integer variables, `WIDTH` and `HEIGHT`, which will be used to establish the size of the frame in pixels.

Following the variable declarations is the constructor method for <u>CustomerGUIOne</u>. This method completely defines what a <u>CustomerGUIOne</u> object is to be. Because a <u>CustomerGUIOne</u> frame is quite simple, we only need to define the frame's title and size—Java takes care of the rest. Finally, the main method is used to instantiate the class. A <u>CustomerGUIOne</u> frame object is created and then displayed using the **show()** method.

Obviously, this frame has no contents, no components. Note that when this application runs, the frame will be positioned in the upper left corner of the screen by default. We will add code later to center the frame on the screen, making it easier for the user to view. Also note that such a frame could be moved manually around the screen by dragging its title bar and may be closed simply by clicking the Close button in the upper right corner. Of course, to make this GUI more interesting and useful, we need to add some components.

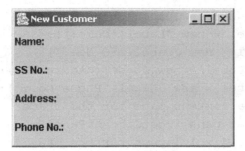

FIGURE **10.4.** GUI with labels only.

JLABEL: ADDING LABELS TO A WINDOW

Labels in a GUI simply provide graphic or textual information to the user. For example, the text "Name:" could be placed as a label next to a text field that allows the user to enter her name. Labels are defined with the JLabel class. A JLabel object displays a single line of text, an image, or both a text and image. The Java code in Listing 10.2 (CustomerGUITwo.java) is used to create the GUI shown in Figure 10.4.

Listing 10.2: `CustomerGUITwo.java`

```
// GUI for bank customer application with labels
import javax.swing.*; // import Swing package
import java.awt.*; // import AWT package
// this class inherits methods from the JFrame class
public class CustomerGUITwo extends JFrame
{
   // static variables to hold frame dimensions in
   // pixels
   private static final int WIDTH = 275;
   private static final int HEIGHT = 170;
   private JLabel nameLabel, ssnLabel, addressLabel,
     phoneLabel;
   public CustomerGUITwo()
   // constructor method defines frame
   {
     setTitle("New Customer");
     // set the title of the frame
```

```
      // instantiate JLabel objects
      nameLabel = new JLabel("Name:");
      ssnLabel = new JLabel("SS No.:");
      addressLabel = new JLabel("Address:");
      phoneLabel = new JLabel("Phone No.:");
      // get a content pane for the frame
      Container pane = getContentPane();
      // set a 4 x 1 layout for the pane
      pane.setLayout(new GridLayout(4,1));
      // add label objects to the pane
      pane.add(nameLabel);
      pane.add(ssnLabel);
      pane.add(addressLabel);
      pane.add(phoneLabel);
      setSize(WIDTH, HEIGHT); // set the frame size
      // call method to center frame on screen
      centerFrameOnScreen(WIDTH, HEIGHT);
   } // end constructor method
public void centerFrameOnScreen(int frameWidth, int
   frameHeight)
   {
      // use the Toolkit and Dimension classes from
      //java.awt
      // create a Toolkit object
      Toolkit aToolkit = Toolkit.getDefaultToolkit();
      // create a Dimension object with user screen
      // information
      Dimension screen = aToolkit.getScreenSize();
      // assign x, y position of upper-left corner of
      // frame
      int xPostionOfFrame = (screen.width -
        frameWidth)/2;
      int yPositionOfFrame = (screen.height -
        frameHeight)/2;
      // method to center frame on user's screen
      setBounds(xPostionOfFrame, yPositionOfFrame,
        frameWidth, frameHeight);
   } // end centerFrameOnScreen() method
public static void main(String [] args)
```

```
   // declare main() method
   {
      // create the frame object
      JFrame aCustomerGUITwo = new CustomerGUITwo();
      aCustomerGUITwo.show(); // display the frame
   } // end main
} // end class
```

The code in Listing 10.2 (`CustomerGUITwo.java`) contains several important new statements. First, we must import the `java.awt` package because we are using the Container class, which is found in this package. Next, we declare four JLabel objects: nameLabel, ssnLabel, addressLabel, and phoneLabel.

The **CustomerGUITwo()** constructor method sets the frame title as before, but then creates the four JLabel objects. Next, a content pane called `pane` is obtained to hold the JLabel objects. In Java, a content pane can be thought of as the inner part of a frame, surrounded by the title bar and the frame borders. It is the content pane that can be formatted to hold the GUI components. Then, the **setLayout()** method of the Container class is used to create a four row, one column rectangular layout to hold the labels.

After the layout is set, the **add()** method of the Container class is used to place the four label objects in the pane. Finally, the size of the frame is set and a method is invoked that centers the frame on the screen, passing WIDTH and HEIGHT to the method. This method for centering the frame again uses the `java.awt` package and some simple arithmetic to accomplish its purpose. The **main()** method then simply creates the frame object and displays it.

While the GUI will indeed be centered on the screen, it still needs more work because it doesn't do anything yet. There are no text fields or buttons. The labels themselves simply appear, one per row within the layout. Next, we will discuss text fields that can be used for data input and output.

JTextField: Adding Text Fields to a Window

A JTextField object is an enclosed area in which the user can enter text or text can be displayed to the user. Ordinarily, data are entered in one or more text fields and the user performs an action, such as clicking a button, to process the data. The class JTextField inherits from class JTextComponent, which provides many features for processing the data. Additionally, you could create a text

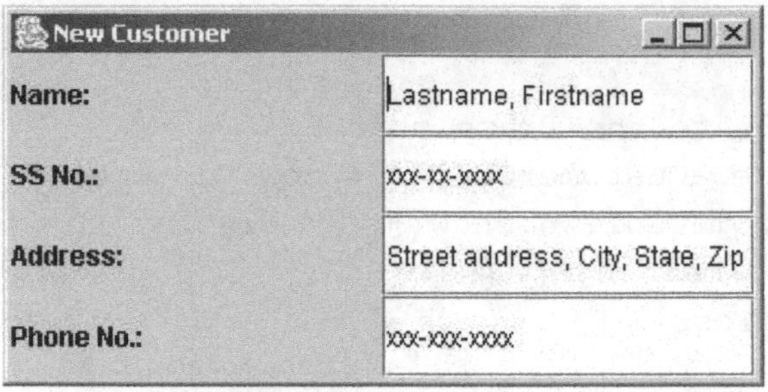

FIGURE **10.5. GUI with labels and text fields only.**

field for passwords (where typed text would appear as a series of *'s) by simply using the JPasswordField class instead of JTextField.

The program in Listing 10.2 is now modified to include text fields and is shown in Listing 10.3. Note that the only additions are four JTextField objects. The resulting GUI is shown in Figure 10.5.

Listing 10.3—`CustomerGUIThree.java`

```
// GUI for bank customer application with labels and
// text fields
import javax.swing.*; // import Swing package
import java.awt.*; // import AWT package
// inherits from the JFrame class

public class CustomerGUIThree extends JFrame
{
   // static variables to hold frame dimensions in
   // pixels
   private static final int WIDTH = 350;
   private static final int HEIGHT = 175;
   // declare JLabel and JTextField objects
   private JLabel nameLabel, ssnLabel, addressLabel,
     phoneLabel;
   private JTextField nameTextField, ssnTextField,
     phoneTextField; addressTextField,
   public CustomerGUIThree()
   // constructor method defines frame
   {
```

```
    setTitle("New Customer");
    // set the title of the frame
    // instantiate JLabel objects
    nameLabel = new JLabel("Name:");
    ssnLabel = new JLabel("SS No.:");
    addressLabel = new JLabel("Address:");
    phoneLabel = new JLabel("Phone No.:");
    // instantiate JTextField objects
    nameTextField = new JTextField("Lastname,
      Firstname", 30);
    ssnTextField = new JTextField("xxx-xx-xxxx", 11);
    addressTextField = new JTextField("Street address,
      City, State, Zip", 40);
    phoneTextField = new JTextField("xxx-xxx-xxxx",
      12);
    // get a content pane for the frame
    Container pane = getContentPane();
    // set a four row, two column layout
    pane.setLayout(new GridLayout(4,2));
    // add JLabel and JTextField objects to the content
    // pane
    pane.add(nameLabel);
    pane.add(nameTextField);
    pane.add(ssnLabel);
    pane.add(ssnTextField);
    pane.add(addressLabel);
    pane.add(addressTextField);
    pane.add(phoneLabel);
    pane.add(phoneTextField);
    setSize(WIDTH, HEIGHT); // set the frame size
    // call method to center frame on screen
    centerFrameOnScreen(WIDTH, HEIGHT);
} // end constructor method
public void centerFrameOnScreen(int frameWidth,
  int frameHeight)
{
    // create a Toolkit object
    Toolkit aToolkit = Toolkit.getDefaultToolkit();
    // create a Dimension object with user screen
```

```
        // information
        Dimension screen = aToolkit.getScreenSize();
        // assign x, y position of upper-left corner of
        // frame
        int xPostionOfFrame = (screen.width -
          frameWidth)/2;
        int yPositionOfFrame = (screen.height -
          frameHeight)/2;
        // method to center frame on user's screen
        setBounds(xPostionOfFrame, yPositionOfFrame,
          frameWidth, frameHeight);
    } // end centerFrameOnScreen() method
    public static void main(String [] args)
    // declare main() method
    {
        // create the frame object
        JFrame aCustomerGUIThree = new CustomerGUIThree();
        aCustomerGUIThree.show(); // display the frame
    } // end main
} // end class
```

Note that the text fields have been pre-loaded with text as a guide to the user for what should be entered and with what format. If preferred, this kind of information could be added to the labels instead, leaving the text fields empty.

The first difference is that the four JTextField objects are declared as private instance variables of the CustomerGUIThree class. In the constructor method, the four JTextField objects are created, including the pre-loaded text referred to earlier. If such text is not desired, the programmer would code the statement as follows, specifying only the field size:

```
nameTextField = new JTextField(30);
```

Note that the frame layout is now 4 rows x 2 columns to accommodate the text fields. Also note that the components are added in order: the name label, then the name text field, and so on (left to right, top to bottom). The remainder of the class is identical to Listing 10.2 (except for the class name, CustomerGUIThree).

The GUI still doesn't do anything. GUI functionality is addressed by the addition of buttons.

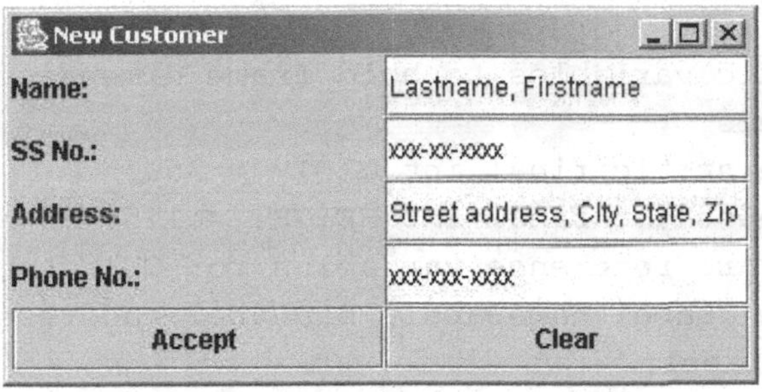

FIGURE **10.6a. GUI resulting from code in Listing 10-4.**

```
Name: Lastname, Firstname

SSN: xxx-xx-xxxx

Address: Street address, City, State, Zip

Phone: xxx-xxx-xxxx
```

FIGURE **10.6b. Output resulting from clicking the Accept button shown in Figure 10.6a.**

JBUTTON: ADDING BUTTONS TO A WINDOW

A button is a component the user clicks to trigger an event. There are many types of Swing buttons (command, check box, toggle, and radio)—a command button is created with class <u>JButton</u>. Listing 10.4 expands the code in Listing 10.3 by adding two buttons with the labels "Accept" and "Clear." Additional code is added to provide functionality for these buttons.

Figure 10.6a shows the resulting GUI while Figure 10.6b shows the output that appears when the "Accept" command button is clicked. (The only "processing" that occurs at this point is sending information to the user.)

Listing 10.4—CustomerGUIFour.java

```java
// GUI for bank customer application with labels,
// text fields, and buttons
import javax.swing.*; // import Swing package
import java.awt.*; // import AWT package
import java.awt.event.*; // import AWT Event package
// this class inherits methods from the JFrame class
public class CustomerGUIFour extends JFrame
```

```
{
    // static variables to hold frame dimensions in
    // pixels
    private static final int WIDTH = 350;
    private static final int HEIGHT = 175;
    // declare reference variables for GUI components
    private JLabel nameLabel, ssnLabel, addressLabel,
      phoneLabel;
    private JTextField nameTextField, ssnTextField,
      addressTextField, phoneTextField;
    private JButton acceptB, clearB;
    // declare reference variables for event handlers
    private AcceptButtonHandler abHandler;
    private ClearButtonHandler cbHandler;
    public CustomerGUIFour()
    // constructor method defines frame
    {
        setTitle("New Customer");
        // set the title of the frame
        // instantiate JLabel objects
        nameLabel = new JLabel("Name:");
        ssnLabel = new JLabel("SS No.:");
        addressLabel = new JLabel("Address:");
        phoneLabel = new JLabel("Phone No.:");
        // instantiate JTextField objects
        nameTextField = new JTextField("Lastname,
          Firstname", 30);
        ssnTextField = new JTextField("xxx-xx-xxxx", 11);
        addressTextField = new JTextField("Street address,
          City, State, Zip", 40);
        phoneTextField = new JTextField("xxx-xxx-xxxx",
          12);
        // instantiate Accept button
        acceptB = new JButton("Accept");
        abHandler = new AcceptButtonHandler();
        acceptB.addActionListener(abHandler);
        // instantiate Clear button
        clearB = new JButton("Clear");
        cbHandler = new ClearButtonHandler();
        clearB.addActionListener(cbHandler);
```

```
    // get a content pane for the frame
    Container pane = getContentPane();
    // five row, two column layout for pane
    pane.setLayout(new GridLayout(5,2));
    // add objects to the content pane
    pane.add(nameLabel);
    pane.add(nameTextField);
    pane.add(ssnLabel);
    pane.add(ssnTextField);
    pane.add(addressLabel);
    pane.add(addressTextField);
    pane.add(phoneLabel);
    pane.add(phoneTextField);
    pane.add(acceptB);
    pane.add(clearB);
    setSize(WIDTH, HEIGHT); // set the frame size
    // call method to center frame on screen
    centerFrameOnScreen(WIDTH, HEIGHT);
} // end constructor method
public void centerFrameOnScreen(int frameWidth,
  int frameHeight)
{
    // use the Toolkit and Dimension classes from
    // java.awt
    // create a Toolkit object
    Toolkit aToolkit = Toolkit.getDefaultToolkit();
    // create a Dimension object with user screen
    // information
    Dimension screen = aToolkit.getScreenSize();
    // assign x, y position of upper-left corner of
    //frame
    int xPostionOfFrame = (screen.width -
      frameWidth)/2;
    int yPositionOfFrame = (screen.height -
      frameHeight)/2;
    // method to center frame on user's screen
    setBounds(xPostionOfFrame, yPositionOfFrame,
      frameWidth, frameHeight);
} // end centerFrameOnScreen() method
private class AcceptButtonHandler implements
```

```
    ActionListener
  {
     public void actionPerformed(ActionEvent e)
     {
        String aName = nameTextField.getText();
        String aSSN = ssnTextField.getText();
        String anAddress = addressTextField.getText();
        String aPhone = phoneTextField.getText();
        Customer aCustomer = new Customer(aName, aSSN,
          anAddress, aPhone);
        System.out.println("Name: " +
          aCustomer.getName());
        System.out.println("SSN: " +
          aCustomer.getSSN());
        System.out.println("Address: " +
          aCustomer.getAddress());
        System.out.println("Phone: " +
          aCustomer.getPhone());
     }
  }
  private class ClearButtonHandler implements
    ActionListener
  {
     public void actionPerformed(ActionEvent e)
     {
        nameTextField.setText("");
        ssnTextField.setText("");
        addressTextField.setText("");
        phoneTextField.setText("");
     }
  }
  public static void main(String [] args)
  // declare main() method
  {
     // create the frame object
     JFrame aCustomerGUIFour = new CustomerGUIFour();
       aCustomerGUIFour.show(); // display the frame
  } // end main
} // end class
```

How Java Handles Events

Buttons add functionality to a GUI. When the user clicks a button, she expects something to happen. In this case, clicking the Accept button should cause information to be displayed to the user and clicking the Clear button should clear the text fields of their contents.

How the Java programmer controls the behavior of buttons should be explained carefully. When a JButton object is clicked, an action event object is created, which sends a message (a method call) to another object, known as an action listener. When the listener receives the message, it performs an action. In order to accomplish all this, the programmer must (1) register (define) a listener for each JButton object and (2) define the methods to be invoked when the listener receives an event.

Java uses the class ActionListener to handle action events. This class is a special kind of Java class known as an interface. Roughly speaking, an interface is a class that contains only method *headings* terminated by semicolons. These special method headings have no body (code)—this is supplied elsewhere by the programmer. The ActionListener interface contains only one method, **actionPerformed()**. Since interface methods have no body, objects from such classes cannot be instantiated. So how do you create an ActionListener object?

To register an action listener for the JButton object acceptB, you first create a class called AcceptButtonHandler which will use (or implement) the ActionListener interface. Then you will write your unique code for an action-Performed method to do the processing required, as shown below:

```
private class AcceptButtonHandler implements
  ActionListener
{
  public void actionPerformed(ActionEvent e)
  {
    // code for required processing when button is
    // clicked
  }
}
```

Note that this special button-handling class (AcceptButtonHandler) is private since only the CustomerGUI class should be allowed to use it. The key word implements is added to utilize the built-in functionality of the ActionListener interface.

What we need to do within our CustomerGUI class is to create an Accept button handler object which will then "listen" for a click of the Accept button. When the click occurs, the appropriate **actionPerformed()** method will be invoked and processing will occur (display the customer information, in this case).

Details of Listing 10.4

We start with the code in Listing 10.3 and begin to make changes. First, we import the `java.awt.event` package to allow us to handle action events. We also declare reference variables for the buttons themselves and for their event handlers.

Within the constructor method for the CustomerGUIFour class, we create the button objects as well as the event-handler objects. Then we enable handler objects to listen for events. The layout for the new GUI is changed to five rows and two columns to accommodate the new buttons. The buttons are then added to the pane.

The AcceptButtonHandler class is then added to the CustomerGUIFour class. This class implements the ActionListener interface and defines an **actionPerformed()** method, which in this case gets the contents of the text fields, creates a Customer object (see the Customer.java class in Listing 3.2), and prints customer information to the user's screen. Likewise, the ClearButtonHandler class simply clears the text from the text fields.

IMPROVING THE WINDOW LAYOUT

This section discusses various types of Java layout managers in the `java.awt` package that allow the programmer to arrange GUI components on a container for improved appearance. Most Java programming environments provide GUI design tools that allow the programmer to graphically design a GUI. The environment then automatically writes the code to create the GUI. However, we will endeavor to write our own code to understand things more fully.

FlowLayout

FlowLayout is the most basic layout manager. When only FlowLayout is used, GUI components are placed on a container from left to right in the order that they are added within the class. If a component will not fit on a line in the container, it is placed on the next line. Class FlowLayout allows GUI components to be left-aligned, centered (the default), or right-aligned. A container's layout is established with method **setLayout()** of class Container, typically before any GUI components are added to the container.

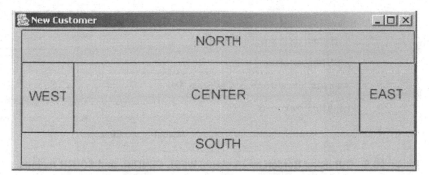

FIGURE **10.7. The five regions of a BorderLayout.**

GridLayout

GridLayout was used previously (see Listing 10.2) to place components neatly within a set of rows and columns, instead of relying on a haphazard left to right, top to bottom arrangement. However, more control is needed for more exact placement of components within a window.

BorderLayout

The BorderLayout manager is used to arrange components into five regions of the content pane: NORTH, SOUTH, EAST, WEST, and CENTER, as illustrated in Figure 10.7. Only one component can be added to each of the five regions of a BorderLayout, but a component can be a container that holds other components. Each region will expand to hold all its contents within the constraints of the overall container size. Additionally, all regions will expand horizontally and vertically to fill the container in the event other regions have no contents (with the exception of an empty CENTER region). For example, if the NORTH and CENTER regions are not used, the WEST and EAST regions will expand horizontally just enough to hold their respective contents (but not necessarily to fill the vacant CENTER) and vertically to fill the vacant NORTH.

There are other Java layout managers, such as BoxLayout and GridBag-Layout, that are more complex but more versatile than those presented here. See, for example, *Java: How to Program* by Deitel and Deitel (see Chapter 1 Bibliography).

The code in Listing 10.5 below, which utilizes both the FlowLayout and BorderLayout classes, produces the GUI shown in Figure 10.8.

Listing 10.5: `CustomerGUIFive.java`

```
// GUI for bank customer application with labels, text
// fields, and buttons--FlowLayout and BorderLayout used
```

FIGURE 10.8. GUI using BorderLayout class, WEST, CENTER, and SOUTH regions.

```java
import javax.swing.*; // import Swing package
import java.awt.*; // import AWT package
import java.awt.event.*; // import AWT Event package
// this class inherits methods from the JFrame class
public class CustomerGUIFive extends JFrame
{
    // static variables to hold frame dimensions in
    // pixels
    private static final int WIDTH = 350;
    private static final int HEIGHT = 175;
    // declare instance variables for GUI components
    private JLabel nameLabel, ssnLabel, addressLabel,
      phoneLabel;
    private JTextField nameTextField, ssnTextField,
      addressTextField, phoneTextField;
    private JButton acceptB, clearB;
    // declare instance variables for button handlers
    private AcceptButtonHandler abHandler;
    private ClearButtonHandler cbHandler;
    public CustomerGUIFive()
    // constructor method defines frame
    {
        setTitle("New Customer");
        // set the title of the frame
        // instantiate JLabel objects
        nameLabel = new JLabel("Name: ",
          SwingConstants.RIGHT);
        ssnLabel = new JLabel("SS No.: ",
          SwingConstants.RIGHT);
```

```
addressLabel = new JLabel("Address: ",
  SwingConstants.RIGHT);
phoneLabel = new JLabel("Phone No.: ",
  SwingConstants.RIGHT);
// instantiate JTextField objects
nameTextField = new JTextField("Lastname,
  Firstname", 30);
ssnTextField = new JTextField("xxx-xx-xxxx", 11);
addressTextField = new JTextField("Street address,
  City, State, Zip", 40);
phoneTextField = new JTextField("xxx-xxx-xxxx",
  12);
// instantiate Accept button
acceptB = new JButton("Accept");
abHandler = new AcceptButtonHandler();
acceptB.addActionListener(abHandler);
// instantiate Clear button
clearB = new JButton("Clear");
cbHandler = new ClearButtonHandler();
clearB.addActionListener(cbHandler);
// get a content pane for the frame
Container pane = getContentPane();
// define a grid and a flow
GridLayout aGrid = new GridLayout(4, 1);
FlowLayout flowRight = new FlowLayout
  (FlowLayout.RIGHT);
// create three panels
JPanel labelPanel = new JPanel();
JPanel textFieldPanel = new JPanel();
JPanel buttonPanel = new JPanel();
// set layouts for panels
labelPanel.setLayout(aGrid, flowRight);
textFieldPanel.setLayout(aGrid);
buttonPanel.setLayout(flowRight);
// add labels to panel
labelPanel.add(nameLabel);
labelPanel.add(ssnLabel);
labelPanel.add(addressLabel);
labelPanel.add(phoneLabel);
```

```java
      // add text fields to panel
      textFieldPanel.add(nameTextField);
      textFieldPanel.add(ssnTextField);
      textFieldPanel.add(addressTextField);
      textFieldPanel.add(phoneTextField);
      // add buttons to panel
      buttonPanel.add(acceptB);
      buttonPanel.add(clearB);
      // add panels to content pane using BorderLayout
      pane.add(labelPanel, BorderLayout.WEST);
      pane.add(textFieldPanel, BorderLayout.CENTER);
      pane.add(buttonPanel, BorderLayout.SOUTH);
      setSize(WIDTH, HEIGHT); // set the frame size
      // call method to center frame on screen
      centerFrameOnScreen(WIDTH, HEIGHT);
   } // end constructor method
   public void centerFrameOnScreen(int frameWidth, int
      frameHeight)
   {
      // use the Toolkit and Dimension classes
      // create a Toolkit object
      Toolkit aToolkit = Toolkit.getDefaultToolkit();
      // create a Dimension object with user screen
      // information
      Dimension screen = aToolkit.getScreenSize();
      // assign x, y position of upper-left corner of
      //frame
      int xPostionOfFrame = (screen.width -
        frameWidth)/2;
      int yPositionOfFrame = (screen.height -
        frameHeight)/2;
      // method to center frame on user's screen
      setBounds(xPostionOfFrame, yPositionOfFrame,
        frameWidth, frameHeight);
   } // end centerFrameOnScreen() method
   private class AcceptButtonHandler implements
     ActionListener
   {
      public void actionPerformed(ActionEvent e)
      {
```

```
            String aName = nameTextField.getText();
            String aSSN = ssnTextField.getText();
            String anAddress = addressTextField.getText();
            String aPhone = phoneTextField.getText();
            Customer aCustomer = new Customer(aName, aSSN,
              anAddress, aPhone);
            System.out.println("Name: " +
              aCustomer.getName());
            System.out.println("SSN: " +
              aCustomer.getSSN());
            System.out.println("Address: " +
              aCustomer.getAddress());
            System.out.println("Phone: " +
              aCustomer.getPhone());
        }
    }
    private class ClearButtonHandler implements
      ActionListener
    {
        public void actionPerformed(ActionEvent e)
        {
            nameTextField.setText("");
            ssnTextField.setText("");
            addressTextField.setText("");
            phoneTextField.setText("");
        }
    }
    public static void main(String [] args)
    // declare main() method
    {
        // create the frame object
        JFrame aCustomerGUIFive = new CustomerGUIFive();
        aCustomerGUIFive.show(); // display the frame
    } // end main
} // end class
```

The constructor method for <u>CustomerGUIFive</u> (Listing 10.5) differs from the one in Listing 10.4 in several important ways. First, the <u>JLabel</u> objects are created with a new parameter, `SwingConstants.RIGHT`. This simply right-aligns the labels within the grid. After the content pane is obtained, a

FIGURE **10.9. GUI using menus.**

FlowLayout object is created to implement a right-alignment of components within a container.

Next, three separate JPanel objects are created (labelPanel, textFieldPanel, and buttonPanel) to allow for more control over component placement within the frame. The layouts for each type of panel are then set (grid for labels and text fields, flow for buttons). After all the labels, text fields, and buttons are added to their respective panels, the panels are in turn added to the desired BorderLayout areas, resulting in the GUI of Figure 10.8.

CREATING DROP-DOWN MENUS

Menus allow users to select a wide variety of actions from a GUI that stills looks small and simple. Menus can be attached to objects from the classes JFrame and JApplet since they contain the **setJMenuBar()** method. Some of the classes used to define menus are JMenuBar, JMenuItem, and JMenu. A menu bar serves as a container for menus. A menu item is a GUI component inside a menu. When a menu item is selected, it causes an action to be performed or another submenu to appear. In the following example, a menu bar is added to our Customer GUI. The File menu has two menu items, Accept and Clear. Selecting these menu items performs the same actions as clicking the Accept and Clear buttons that also appear in the GUI. A Help menu also appears in the menu bar but does nothing in this example. The resulting GUI can be seen in Figure 10.9.

Listing 10.6—`CustomerGUISix.java`

```
// GUI for bank customer application with labels, text
// fields, and buttons
```

```java
import javax.swing.*; // import Swing package
import java.awt.*; // import AWT package
import java.awt.event.*; // import AWT Event package
// this class inherits methods from the JFrame class
public class CustomerGUISix extends JFrame
{
  // static variables to hold frame dimensions in
  // pixels
  private static final int WIDTH = 350;
  private static final int HEIGHT = 175;
  // declare instance variables for GUI components
  private JLabel nameLabel, ssnLabel, addressLabel,
    phoneLabel;
  private JTextField nameTextField, ssnTextField,
    addressTextField, phoneTextField;
  private JButton acceptB, clearB;
  // declare instance variables for button handlers
  private AcceptButtonHandler abHandler;
  private ClearButtonHandler cbHandler;
  public CustomerGUISix()
  // constructor method defines frame
  {
    setTitle("New Customer");
    // set the title of the frame
    // instantiate JLabel objects
    nameLabel = new JLabel("Name: ",
      SwingConstants.RIGHT);
    ssnLabel = new JLabel("SS No.: ",
      SwingConstants.RIGHT);
    addressLabel = new JLabel("Address: ",
      SwingConstants.RIGHT);
    phoneLabel = new JLabel("Phone No.: ",
      SwingConstants.RIGHT);
    // instantiate JTextField objects
    nameTextField = new JTextField("Lastname,
      Firstname", 30);
    ssnTextField = new JTextField("xxx-xx-xxxx",
      11);
    addressTextField = new JTextField("Street address,
      City, State, Zip", 40);
```

```
phoneTextField = new JTextField("xxx-xxx-xxxx",12);
// instantiate Accept button
acceptB = new JButton("Accept");
abHandler = new AcceptButtonHandler();
acceptB.addActionListener(abHandler);
// instantiate Clear button
clearB = new JButton("Clear");
cbHandler = new ClearButtonHandler();
clearB.addActionListener(cbHandler);
// create two JMenu objects with mnemonics
JMenu fileMenu = new JMenu("File");
fileMenu.setMnemonic('F');
JMenu helpMenu = new JMenu("Help");
helpMenu.setMnemonic('H');
// create and add two JMenuItem objects with
// mnemonics and action listeners
JMenuItem acceptItem = new JMenuItem("Accept");
acceptItem.setMnemonic('A');
acceptItem.addActionListener(abHandler);
fileMenu.add(acceptItem);
JMenuItem clearItem = new JMenuItem("Clear");
clearItem.setMnemonic('C');
clearItem.addActionListener(cbHandler);
fileMenu.add(clearItem);
// create a JMenuBar object, set it, add menus
JMenuBar bar = new JMenuBar();
setJMenuBar(bar);
bar.add(fileMenu);
bar.add(helpMenu);
// get a content pane for the frame
Container pane = getContentPane();
// define a grid and a flow
GridLayout aGrid = new GridLayout(4, 1);
FlowLayout flowRight = new FlowLayout
  (FlowLayout.RIGHT);
// create three panels
JPanel labelPanel = new JPanel();
JPanel textFieldPanel = new JPanel();
JPanel buttonPanel = new JPanel();
```

```
      // set layouts for panels
      labelPanel.setLayout(aGrid);
      textFieldPanel.setLayout(aGrid);
      buttonPanel.setLayout(flowRight);
      // add labels to panel
      labelPanel.add(nameLabel);
      labelPanel.add(ssnLabel);
      labelPanel.add(addressLabel);
      labelPanel.add(phoneLabel);
      // add text fields to panel
      textFieldPanel.add(nameTextField);
      textFieldPanel.add(ssnTextField);
      textFieldPanel.add(addressTextField);
      textFieldPanel.add(phoneTextField);

      // add buttons to panel
      buttonPanel.add(acceptB);
      buttonPanel.add(clearB);
      // add panels to content pane using BorderLayout
      pane.add(labelPanel, BorderLayout.WEST);
      pane.add(textFieldPanel, BorderLayout.CENTER);
      pane.add(buttonPanel, BorderLayout.SOUTH);
      setSize(WIDTH, HEIGHT); // set the frame size
      // call method to center frame on screen
      centerFrameOnScreen(WIDTH, HEIGHT);
   } // end constructor method
   public void centerFrameOnScreen(int frameWidth,
     int frameHeight)
   {
      // use the Toolkit and Dimension classes
      // create a Toolkit object
      Toolkit aToolkit = Toolkit.getDefaultToolkit();
      // create a Dimension object with user screen
      // information
      Dimension screen = aToolkit.getScreenSize();
      // assign x, y position of upper-left corner of
      // frame
      int xPostionOfFrame = (screen.width -
        frameWidth)/2;
```

```java
    int yPositionOfFrame = (screen.height -
      frameHeight)/2;
    // method to center frame on user's screen
    setBounds(xPostionOfFrame, yPositionOfFrame,
      frameWidth, frameHeight);
} // end centerFrameOnScreen() method
private class AcceptButtonHandler implements
  ActionListener
{
    public void actionPerformed(ActionEvent e)
    {
      String aName = nameTextField.getText();
      String aSSN = ssnTextField.getText();
      String anAddress = addressTextField.getText();
      String aPhone = phoneTextField.getText();
      Customer aCustomer = new Customer(aName, aSSN,
        anAddress, aPhone);
      System.out.println("Name: " +
        aCustomer.getName());
      System.out.println("SSN: " +
        aCustomer.getSSN());
      System.out.println("Address: " +
        aCustomer.getAddress());
      System.out.println("Phone: " +
        aCustomer.getPhone());
    }
}
private class ClearButtonHandler implements
  ActionListener
{
    public void actionPerformed(ActionEvent e)
    {
      nameTextField.setText("");
      ssnTextField.setText("");
      addressTextField.setText("");
      phoneTextField.setText("");
    }
}
```

```
   public static void main(String [] args) // declare
     // main() method
   {
       // create the frame object
       JFrame aCustomerGUISix = new CustomerGUISix();
       aCustomerGUISix.show(); // display the frame
   } // end main
} // end class
```

All the new code for this program can again be found in the constructor method for the <u>CustomerGUISix</u> class. After the label, text field, and button objects are created, a <u>JMenu</u> object called fileMenu is created. Its mnemonic is set to 'F' so that the user could press Alt-F instead of clicking the word File. The same steps are performed for the Help menu.

After the <u>JMenu</u> objects are created, two <u>JMenuItem</u> objects are instantiated for the object fileMenu:acceptItem and clearItem. The mnemonics 'A' and 'C' are also created so the user can simply press 'A' or 'C' on the keyboard to trigger the desired event. Action listeners are then added for these two <u>JMenuItem</u> objects and they are added to fileMenu.

Finally, a <u>JMenuBar</u> object is created and is set within the frame. Following this, the two <u>JMenu</u> objects, fileMenu and helpMenu, are added to the menu bar. The remainder of the program is unchanged. When the menu items 'Accept' and 'Clear' are selected (using either the mouse or the keyboard), the event handlers will swing into action just the same as if the 'Accept' and 'Clear' buttons had been clicked by the user.

WRITING APPLETS

A Java applet is simply a Java program that runs under control of another program such as a viewer or web browser. The applet is a smaller program with limited capability, a diminished application, thus Java programmers use the diminutive suffix "-let." Some argue that the primary reason for Java's popularity is that it can be used to write applets. Our view, however is that applets are only one of many reasons for Java's widespread usage.

The diminished capability of an applet is deliberately imposed to heighten security on the user's workstation. Applets are typically downloaded from another system, and to restrict malevolent acts, applets cannot access files, except on their host server. In addition, applets do not have a title bar so we cannot attach drop-down menus.

To run an applet, we place an applet HTML tag in a web page. This tag identifies the applet class name and specifies the size of the applet window to appear on the web page. Here, we are going to convert `CustomerGUIFour.java` (Listing 10.4) to an applet named `CustomerGUI.java`. The class file is named `CustomerGUI.class`, and the HTML element is:

```
<APPLET
   CODE = "NewCustomerApplet.class"
   WIDTH = 400 HEIGHT = 200 >
<APPLET>
```

When the web browser encounters this element, it loads and executes the applet.

An applet and an application are quite similar. Here we point out the differences as we convert `CustomerGUIFour.java` to `CustomerGUI.java`.

1. Applets extend the <u>JApplet</u> class instead of extending the <u>JFrame</u> class.
   `public class CustomerGUI extends JApplet`
2. Applets do not have a **main()** method. **main()** simply disappears. In `CustomerGUIFour.java`, our **main()** method did only three things:
   • Create an instance of <u>CustomerGUIFour</u>
   • Establish the window size
   • Make the window visible
   The web browser does all of this for us. It creates the window, makes it the size indicated in the `<APPLET>` element, and makes it visible, thus eliminating the need for our main method.
3. Applets do not have a constructor method—instead we place the constructor code in a method named **init()** that is automatically called when the applet is loaded by the browser. To make the change we merely change the constructor method's name to **init()** and add the return type `void`.
   `public void init () // replaces constructor method`
   Using a web browser, <u>CustomerGUI</u> window appears as shown in Figure 10.10.

What is significant here is that, if we wish, we can now enter customer information from any connected workstation using the applet. From a user's perspective, the applet functions exactly like the application.

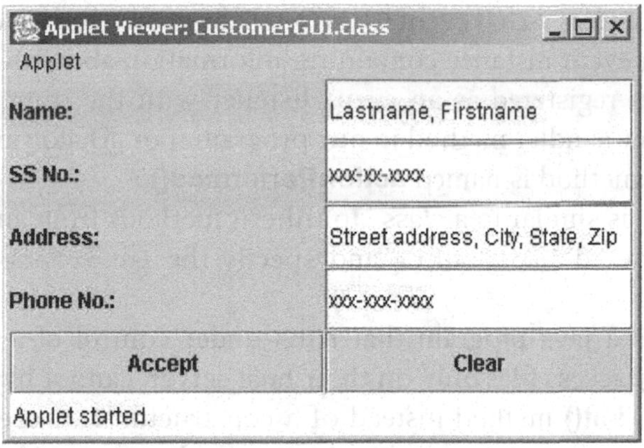

FIGURE 10.10. Customer GUI resulting from an applet.

SUMMARY OF KEY POINTS IN CHAPTER 10

1. Java includes several class libraries called packages. The `java.awt` and `javax.swing` packages contain classes used to create GUIs.
2. A <u>JFrame</u> is a Java GUI component (window) to which we can add other GUI components such as <u>JButton</u>, <u>JLabel</u>, <u>JMenuItem</u>, and <u>JTextField</u>.
3. Both menu events and button events cause the method **actionPerformed()** to be called. Window events cause one of several window event methods to be called, depending on the specific event. For example, closing the window causes **windowClosing()** to be called.
4. Java uses Layout Managers to help arrange GUI components:
   - <u>FlowLayout</u> places components in successive rows. This is the default manager for the <u>JPanel</u> and <u>JApplet</u> classes.
   - <u>BorderLayout</u> places components in the borders and center (NORTH, SOUTH, EAST, WEST, and CENTER). This is the default manager for the <u>JFrame</u> class.
   - <u>GridLayout</u> arranges components in a rectangular grid. The programmer specifies the number of rows and columns.
   - <u>BoxLayout</u> allows GUI components to be arranged left-to-right or top-to-bottom in a container.
   - <u>GridBagLayout</u> is similar to <u>GridLayout</u>, but component size can vary and components can be added in any order.
5. <u>JPanel</u> objects are invisible GUI components that we place in a <u>JFrame</u> to hold other GUI components.

6. When Java detects a GUI event, such as clicking on a button or menu item, it creates an event instance containing information about the event. If our program has registered as an event listener with the source object, Java calls an event handler method in our program. For JButton and JMenuItem objects this method is named **actionPerformed()**.
7. An interface is similar to a class. To inherit methods from an interface, we use the keyword implements and specify the interface_name in the class header.
8. An applet is a Java program that runs under control of a web browser. Applets may access files only on their host server, cannot have menu bars, and have an **init()** method instead of a constructor. However, applets can run on any workstation that has access to the server where the applet and its corresponding web page reside. The applet is downloaded to the workstation from the server along with the web page.

CHAPTER 11

Object-Oriented Development Issues

OBJECTIVES

In this chapter you will study:

- OO development;
- OO analysis and design issues; and
- Technology architecture issues.

This chapter provides an overview of OO development and some of the issues you should consider when developing OO systems. Whereas the previous chapters introduced specific programming topics, this chapter will pull together several of those topics and present them in terms of software development. As you will see, OO development is much more than writing Java programs. The successful software developer must become familiar with, and apply, OO development techniques. OO requires more attention to analysis and design than traditional development; however, the payoff is software that is developed quicker and is easier to maintain. The chapter begins with an overview of OO development followed by a brief introduction to current OO systems development methodologies. Next, activities commonly associated with analysis are presented. Then, various aspects of design necessary for understanding OO development and successful Java programming are discussed. Java examples are provided to enable you to compare and contrast some of the basic philosophical differences between OO and traditional development approaches.

This chapter assumes you understand the following:

Java:
OO concepts (Chapter 2)
Java program structure (Chapter 3)
Defining data (Chapter 4)
Arithmetic (Chapter 5)
Decision making (Chapter 6)
Looping (Chapter 7)
Arrays (Chapter 8)
Data access (Chapter 9)
Graphical User Interfaces (Chapter 10)

DEVELOPING OBJECT-ORIENTED SYSTEMS

Programming is not a stand-alone process, although that has been the focus so far in this book. Writing code is only one part, albeit an important part, of software development. From a life cycle perspective, OO development is quite similar to traditional development. You still must do analysis, design, and programming to create a system, although the precise details and execution of these three phases vary. Until now, we have deliberately focused on OO programming to give you a broad understanding of Java. This chapter gives you an overview of some development issues you should consider in addition to programming.

By now, you have undoubtedly accepted the truth of a statement we made earlier in Chapter 2:

OO is a new way of thinking about the development of systems—it is not simply a programming technique.

In other words, don't view Java programming too narrowly. It is not sufficient for you to understand only the structure and syntax of Java. To successfully develop OO systems, you must also understand OO development including OO analysis and design.

Like all systems development efforts, good analysis and design are essential to the success of the effort. However, where structured development permits us to bypass analysis and design and jump right to coding (essentially a code-and-fix-it development process), the OO paradigm requires us to do analysis and design. We can't simply begin writing code without having previously identified and defined our OO classes.

Class programs are the physical representation of classes identified in analysis and defined in design. Without proper analysis and design, it becomes essentially impossible to know about the programs we must write. The analysis, design, and programming phases are much more closely tied together in OO development than in traditional development. Under traditional structured design, programs have little resemblance to their design documents such as data flow diagrams and system flowcharts. In contrast, the OO design documents clearly indicate the class programs that are needed.

OO METHODOLOGIES

Adhering to the analysis, design, and programming phases, however, does not guarantee that we will produce good systems. Our projects must also follow an established formal systems development methodology (SDM). An SDM is a detailed guide for the development of a system, sort of a "how to" book for developing systems.

Chapter 2 introduced UML and class diagrams. UML consists of several additional diagrams, including sequence, collaboration, activity, component, package, deployment, and state diagrams, and use case models. As indicated in Chapter 2, UML is really a notation set for OO modeling. However, UML is not an SDM.

It is significant that the Object Management Group (OMG) has adopted the UML notation set. UML has thus become a standard notation set for OO development, and future OO SDMs are expected to utilize UML. Although a detailed explanation of UML diagrams is outside the scope of this book, we encourage you to familiarize yourself with UML before getting too far into OO development.

One of the first methodologies to take full advantage of the UML notation is the Rational Unified Process (RUP) developed and published by Rational Corporation (the originators of UML). Books describing the "unified process" (the RUP and other generic versions) are now available. (See Bibliography at end of this chapter.)

The Object-Oriented Process, Environment, and Notation (OPEN) methodology is another recent OO methodology, developed by a consortium of over 35 members. According to the authors of the book detailing OPEN, it "may be used in conjunction with any object-oriented method or notation, such as Coad, Firesmith, Odell, SOMA, or UML."

There are several additional OO methodologies, including the Object Modeling Technique (OMT), Fusion, Coad's methodology, and Martin and Odells methodology. Additionally, several commercial OO methodologies are available. Some of these use UML, and others do not.

Among the myriad of methodologies, you will find differences in basic development philosophies, phase activities, sequence of phases, and deliverables. Some suggest an iterative approach utilizing prototyping and incremental class development, while others propose a more sequential technique. In addition to specific OO methodologies, many other new developments, such as the Agile Methodology, eXtreme Programming, DSDM, and SCRUM, have taken center stage in an effort to streamline the software development process. These new processes often address, overlap, and complement OO methodologies.

Which methodology is best? Unfortunately, there is not an easy answer to this question. Hopefully, in time, the available methodologies will become more compatible, thereby making the question easier to answer.

OO ANALYSIS

In OO analysis, the objective is to determine user needs and then model these requirements. This should sound familiar because you probably do the same things now. There are several ways to model requirements using UML. Use case models, class diagrams, sequence diagrams, collaboration diagrams, state diagrams, and activity diagrams are all used to model user requirements. Of these, the class diagram is the most important because everything revolves around classes. The other diagrams all provide input to the class diagram.

Our focus during analysis is to understand the business logic (problem domain) of the system. The class diagram identifies the classes we need and their relationships to each other. The use cases provide scenarios of requirements (e.g., what are the steps needed to open a checking account?). Sequence diagrams illustrate interaction between the classes by modeling calls to various methods.

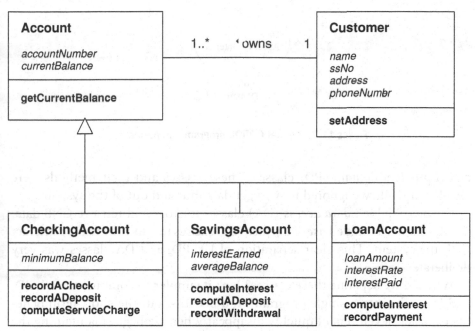

FIGURE 11.1. Class diagram for Community National Bank.

Overall, we want to know how the business works and what it will take to solve the users' problems. In our Community National Bank example, the class diagram depicts accounts, checking accounts, and customers (Figure 11.1). Specific user interfaces and data details are delayed until the design phase.

OO DESIGN

In OO design, the models created during analysis are enhanced to provide more detail. Among other things, specifications are provided for the user interface and data access aspects of the system. Additional UML models such as package diagrams, component diagrams, and deployment diagrams become useful during the design phase of development.

With the exception of Chapters 9 (Data Access) and 10 (GUI), this book has focused on the specific business logic for the Community National Bank. We developed classes to model accounts and customers, and methods to post checks, post deposits, and compute service charges. The various <u>Account</u> and <u>Customer</u> classes representing the heart of the business processing logic are

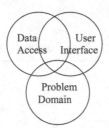

FIGURE 11.2. Typical COBOL program components.

called *problem domain* (PD) classes. These classes and their methods were developed while we ignored how to get data into and out of the system.

Chapter 9 added *data access* (DA) classes to store and retrieve CNB data. Then, Chapter 10 added *user interface* (UI) classes to allow the user to interact with the system. This clear separation of UI, PD, and DA classes was very deliberate.

Why did we separate these classes? Isn't it simpler to combine the UI, PD, and DA tasks into a single program? You bet it is, but the short-term benefits of easier development quickly disappear when we begin maintaining the system. Good design, whether OO or structured, suggests that we decompose processing into *small independent* modules. We want each program to be unaffected by changes to other programs in the system.

In the early days of COBOL, we wrote large programs that did numerous, sometimes unrelated, processing tasks. Specifically, we wrote programs that included a user interface, problem domain processing, and data access all in one program. The interface, processing, and data access functions were not separated and were not independent. Processing tended to be sequential with the code reflecting the sequence of execution rather than a logical partitioning of the code. Figure 11.2 illustrates these three components graphically.

Why worry about separating these three components? On the surface, it makes sense to keep the three together. For example, if we want to post checks to checking accounts, we will input account number and check amount, retrieve the appropriate checking account record, subtract the amount of the check from the account balance, and then rewrite the record back. Why not put all of these tasks in one program? The answer is simple: a change in any one of the three areas (UI-PD-DA) will force us to recompile and test the *entire program*. For example, if we switch from a text-based user interface to a GUI, then the monolithic program must be changed and recompiled in total. Specifically, we will need to first locate all of the UI code, replace it

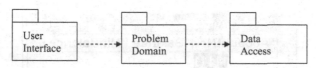

FIGURE 11.3. Package diagram.

with the new interface code, then recompile and test the program. It is likely when we wrote the original program we tied the UI to the problem domain processing and data access code, making it difficult to locate and make all of the changes needed to convert to a GUI front end.

For another example, consider the impact of changing the data file structure. We may, for example, add a field or change from an indexed file to a relational database. Parts of the program would have to be changed and recompiled. No problem, right? **Wrong!** How many times have you made a change in one area of a program, only to find that the change you made caused unanticipated problems in another part of the program or system? If this has happened to you, then you have experienced the problems associated with overlapping the three components. By separating these components, we are essentially isolating program functions and reducing future maintenance problems.

THREE-TIER DESIGN

Separating UI, DA, and PD is often referred to as *three-tier design* (not to be confused with "three-tier architecture" to be discussed later). The three-tier design can be illustrated using UML package diagrams (Figure 11.3). Package diagrams provide a logical grouping of classes. In the following example, three packages are shown: user interface, problem domain, and data access. Packages are represented by a symbol resembling a file folder. A dashed line is used to show dependency among packages.

Let's demonstrate Java three-tiered design by developing a small system for Community National Bank to post checks to customer checking accounts. This system will have four class programs:

1. `PostChecksGUI.java`—a GUI window to permit the user to input account number and check amount.
2. `Account.java`—the same class program developed way back in Chapter 3.

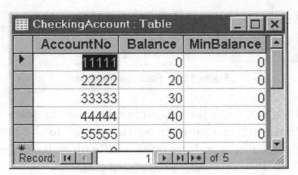

FIGURE 11.4. CheckingAccount database table.

3. CheckingAccount**PD**.java—the result of modifying CheckingAccount.java from Chapter 3 to interface with the data access class.
4. CheckingAccount**DA**.java—a new class program to provide data access using a relational database.

This example will use a Microsoft Access relational database, but the data access class effectively hides the data storage implementation from all the other classes. The UI and PD classes are totally insulated from the database.

First, we create a relational database with the five accounts shown in Figure 11.4:

Next, we design the data access class program, CheckingAccount**DA**.java, modeling it after the DataBaseDemo.java program we developed in Chapter 9. CheckingAccount**DA**.java will have four class methods:

1. **initialize()**—establishes the database connection
2. **terminate()**—closes the database connection
3. **getAccount()**—retrieves the specified account
4. **updateAccount()**—stores the account with a new balance

We then add three new class methods to our problem domain class, CheckingAccount**PD**.java:

1. **initialize()**—calls **initialize()** in the data access class
2. **terminate()**—calls **terminate()** in the data access class

3. **recordACheck()**—calls **getAccount()** in the data access class and, if the account is found, call the instance method. (We will also have the **recordACheck()** instance method).

We will also make two modifications to the instance method **record-ACheck()**:

1. Throw <u>NSFException</u> if the account does not have sufficient funds to pay the check.
2. Call **updateAccount()** in CheckingAccount**DA**.java to store the updated account balance in the database.

When multiple classes are interacting, one of the best ways to depict the communication between classes is the UML *sequence diagram*. Sequence diagrams, part of the UML notation package, illustrate the timing and sequence of messages between classes and objects. They also depict various scenarios of the system (e.g., scenarios identified from use cases). Examples of scenarios from Community National Bank include opening an account, closing an account, recording checks, and recording deposits.

Each object and/or class is identified at the top of the diagram using the following naming convention:

```
Object:Class     represents an object from a class
      :Class     represents a class (no object)
```

Arrowed lines are used to show the interaction between the objects and classes. Solid lines indicate the message and arguments sent (in parentheses). Dashed lines indicate variables returned. The non-arrow end of the line marks the sender of the message; the arrowed end shows the receiver of the message. The ordering of the arrowed lines indicates the timing and sequence of interaction. The vertical line beneath each object and class represents the timeline.

Figure 11.5 shows the sequence diagram for recording checks. In this case, it maps the interaction between the GUI, problem domain, and data access classes. Specifically, the <u>PostChecksGUI</u>, <u>CheckingAccountPD</u>, and <u>CheckingAccountDA</u> classes are used; a <u>CheckingAccountPD</u> object, named anAccount, is also used. Note the shaded names at the top of Figure 11.5 are

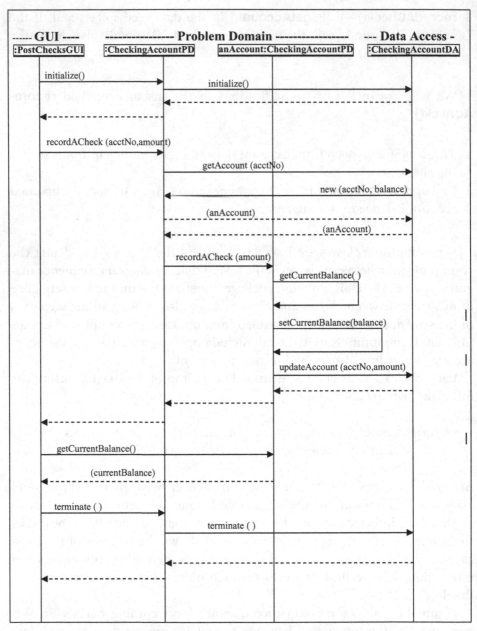

FIGURE 11.5. Sequence diagram for recording checks.

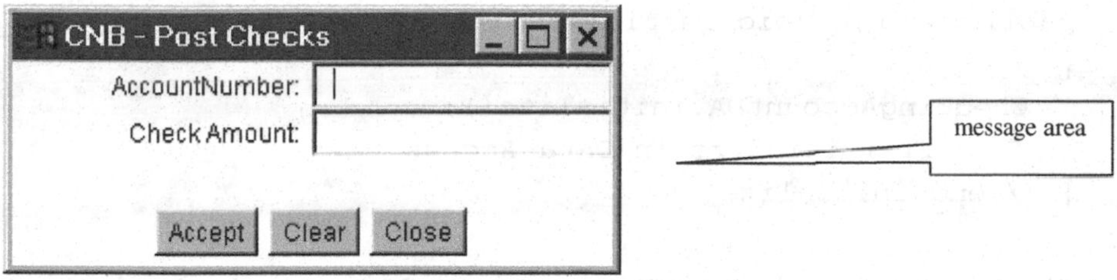

message area

FIGURE 11.6. Post checks window.

not part of the sequence diagram; we have included them here to highlight the UI, PD, and DA objects and classes.

The sequence diagram in Figure 11.5 shows the normal course of events for recording checks. Unusual occurrences such as overdrawn accounts or invalid account numbers are not represented on this sequence diagram. Alternate sequence diagrams can be created to demonstrate the sequence of events that occur when an exception is thrown.

The GUI window displayed by `PostChecksGUI.java` is shown in Figure 11.6.

The **main()** method in `PostChecksGUI.java` creates and displays the window, then it calls the class method **initialize()** in `CheckingAccountPD.java`.

```
public static void main(String args[])
// main method called first
{
   // create window object
   PostChecksGUI aWindow = new PostChecksGUI();
   aWindow.setSize(300,170);
      // pixels wide x pixels high
   aWindow.show();               // display the window
   CheckingAccountPD.initialize();
      // initialize data manager
} // end of main method
```

The **initialize()** method in the PD class, CheckingAccountPD, simply calls **initialize()** in the DA class, CheckingAccountDA.

```
public static void initialize()
{
   CheckingAccountDA.initialize();
   // call initialize in Data Access
} // end initialize
```

The **initialize()** method in CheckingAccountDA.java loads the database driver, then creates a connection and statement object. We could do this each time we get an account but it is more efficient to do it once when we begin processing.

```
public static void initialize() // initialize method
{
   try
   { // load the jdbc - odbc bridge driver for
     // Windows-95
   Class.forName("sun.jdbc.odbc.JdbcOdbcDriver");
   // create connection object
   aConnection = DriverManager.getConnection(url,
   // "Admin", "JavaIsFun");
   // create statement object
   aStatement = aConnection.createStatement();
   } // end try
   catch (Exception e)
   {
      System.out.println("Exception caught "+ e);
   }
} // end initialize
```

When the user enters the account number and check amount in the GUI window and clicks the Accept button, PostChecksGUI.java first validates the input data, then calls the class method **recordACheck()** in CheckingAccountPD.java. This method can throw two different exceptions: NoAccountFoundException and NSFException. If either of these is thrown, the GUI class catches them and displays the appropriate error message in the message area of the GUI window. If no exceptions are caught, the resulting account balance is displayed in the message area. The PostChecksGUI.java code is:

```
public void postCheck()
{
    try
    {
        anAccount = CheckingAccountPD.recordACheck
            (accountNumber, checkAmount);
        lblMessage.setText("Balance is: " + Float.toString
            (anAccount.getCurrentBalance()));
    }
    catch (NoAccountFoundException e)
    {
        lblMessage.setText("No Account Found");
    }
    catch (NSFException e)
    {
        lblMessage.setText("Insufficient Funds");
    }
} // end postCheck
```

The class method **recordACheck()** in `CheckingAccountPD.java` first calls **getAccount()** in the DA class to retrieve the account entered by the user.

```
// note this is a class method - we also have an
// instance method with
// this name
public static CheckingAccountPD recordACheck (int
  accountNumber,
    float checkAmount) throws NoAccountFoundException,
      NSFException
{
    try
    { // ask Data Access class to get the account
      // object for us
      CheckingAccountPD anAccount =
        CheckingAccountDA.getAccount (accountNumber);
      // if successful, post check
      anAccount.recordACheck(checkAmount);
      return anAccount; // return the object reference
      // variable
```

```
    }
    catch (NoAccountFoundException e) // no account found
    {
       throw e;
    }
    catch (NSFException e)    // not sufficient funds
    {
       throw e;
    }
} // end class method recordACheck
```

If the account is successfully retrieved, **getAccount()** creates a CheckingAccount object and returns the reference variable anAccount to the PD class. Note that if **getAccount()** cannot retrieve the account, a NoAccountFoundException is thrown by the DA class.

```
public static CheckingAccountPD getAccount(int acctNo)
   throws
   NoAccountFoundException
{
   try
   {
      String sqlQuery = "SELECT AccountNo, Balance,
        MinBalance
         FROM CheckingAccount WHERE AccountNo
           =" + acctNo;
      // execute the SQL query
      rs = aStatement.executeQuery(sqlQuery);
      boolean more = rs.next(); // set the cursor
      if (more)
      { // if we got the account extract the data &
        // display
         int acctNO = rs.getInt(1);
         float balance = rs.getFloat(2);
         float minBalance = rs.getFloat(3);
         //create object
         anAccount = new CheckingAccountPD(acctNO,
           balance);
      }
      else
```

```
      { // no account found - create & throw the
        // exception
        NoAccountFoundException e = new
           NoAccountFoundException("Not Found");
        throw e;
      } // end if
    } // end try
    catch (SQLException e)
    {
      while (e != null)
      // we can have multiple exceptions here
      {
        System.out.println("SQLException caught "+ e);
        e = e.getNextException();
      } // end while loop
    } // end catch
    return anAccount;
  } // end getAccount
```

The **recordACheck()** method in the problem domain calls its *instance* method **recordACheck()** to actually post the check to the account object. The instance method **recordACheck()** will throw an NSFException if the account does not have sufficient funds to pay the check.

```
// instance method to post a check to this account
public void recordACheck (float checkAmount) throws
  NSFException
{
   float currentBalance = getCurrentBalance();
   // get current balance
   if (currentBalance >= checkAmount)
   // see if sufficient funds
   {
     currentBalance = currentBalance - checkAmount;
     setCurrentBalance(currentBalance);
     // set current balance
     // update the balance in the database
     CheckingAccountDA.updateAccount(getAccountNumber(),
        currentBalance);
   }
```

```
    else
    { // if not, throw an exception
      NSFException e = new NSFException("Not Sufficient
        Funds");
      throw e;
    } // end if
} // end instance method recordACheck
```

If there are sufficient funds to pay the check, the class method **update-Account()** in the DA class is called to store the new balance in the database.

```
public static void updateAccount(int acctNo, float
  balance)
{
    try
    {
      String sqlUpdate = "UPDATE CheckingAccount SET
        Balance = " + balance +" WHERE AccountNo = " +
        acctNo;
      aStatement.executeUpdate(sqlUpdate);
    } // end try
    catch (SQLException e)
    {
      while (e != null) // we can have multiple
        exceptions here
      {
        System.out.println("SQLException caught "+ e);
        e = e.getNextException();
      } // end while loop
    } // end catch
} // end update
```

The interaction of multiple objects and classes can get confusing. Sequence diagrams and written narratives can help eliminate the confusion by outlining the interaction. It may be helpful at this time to go back and look at the sequence diagram again and reread the Java code. The following narrative summarizes the interaction:

Summary Narrative for Recording Checks

1. PostChecksGUI creates and displays the window, then calls the class method **initialize()** in CheckingAccountPD.
2. The **initialize()** method in CheckingAccountPD calls **initialize()** in: CheckingAccountDA to create the database connection.
3. The **initialize()** method in CheckingAccountDA loads the database driver, then creates a connection and statement object. We could do this each time we get an account but it is more efficient to do it once when we begin processing.
4. The user enters the account number and check amount in the GUI window and clicks the Accept button. PostChecksGUI validates the input data, then calls the class method **recordACheck()** in CheckingAccountPD. This method can throw two different exceptions: NoAccountFoundException and NSFException. If either of these is thrown, the GUI class catches them and displays the appropriate error message in the message area of the GUI window.
5. The class method **recordACheck()** in CheckingAccountPD calls **getAccount()** in CheckingAccountDA to retrieve the account entered by the user.
6. If the account is successfully retrieved, **getAccount()** creates a CheckingAccount object by calling the constructor method in CheckingAccountPD; a reference to the new Account object, an-Account, is returned to CheckingAccountDA. This reference variable is then returned to the CheckingAccountPD, the initiator of this sequence of events. If **getAccount()** cannot retrieve the account, a NoAccountFoundException is thrown by CheckingAccountDA.
7. CheckingAccountPD calls its instance method **recordACheck()** to actually post the check to the account object. The **recordACheck()** method then does three things: (1) calls **getCurrentBalance()** to retrieve the current balance; (2) subtracts the check amount from the current balance and calls **setCurrentBalance()** to set the balance. If there are sufficient funds to pay the check, the class method **updateAccount()** in CheckingAccountDA is called to store the new balance in the database. The instance method **recordACheck()** will throw an NSFException if the account does not have sufficient funds to pay the check.
8. When the user clicks the Close button, the class method **terminate()** in CheckingAccountPD is called. This method, in turn, calls **terminate()** in CheckingAccountDA to close the database connection.

The complete programs are included at the Cambridge University Press web site (http://www.cup.org/), and we encourage you to experiment with them. An excellent exercise is to modify the GUI window to also post deposits. You will need to write the **recordADeposit()** class method for Checking-Account`PD`.`java`, but you should not make any changes to the data access class.

ARCHITECTURE ISSUES

At some point in the design, hopefully as late as possible, decisions will be made regarding the technology architecture. Specifically, issues such as platform type and number of tiers are addressed. Consideration must be given to single machine, two-tier, three-tier, or n-tiered architectures. An important OO design issue is the physical location of the classes. For single machine architecture, the answer is simple: all classes reside on the machine. For two-tiered client-server systems, there are several options. One option is to put the user interface and problem domain classes on the client and put data access on the server. For a three-tiered system that normally contains a client, an intermediate server, and a back end or host server, several options are also available. For example, we can put the user interface on the client, problem domain on the intermediate server, and data access on the back end. For Internet applications, which may be n-tiered, it is possible for all classes to be on the server until the user activates the browser, which then downloads the user interface, problem domain, and data access as needed.

UML provides notation to illustrate the physical distribution of objects. Deployment diagrams are useful in showing the physical location of objects, groups of objects (*packages*), or portions of objects (*components*). An example of a deployment diagram, for the Community National Bank problem, is shown in Figure 11.7. In this case, the user interface is located on the bank teller's PC which is connected via a token ring network to an AS/400 located in the bank, which in turn is connected to the home office's mainframe via a T1 line. The user interface, problem domain, and data access packages are stored on these three tiers respectively.

The physical allocation of objects to different platforms requires some mechanism for passing objects and messages between objects across the tiers. The mechanism for accomplishing this task is called an *object request broker* (ORB). An ORB keeps track of object locations and provides the communication mechanisms to allow objects to communicate. Basically, the ORB

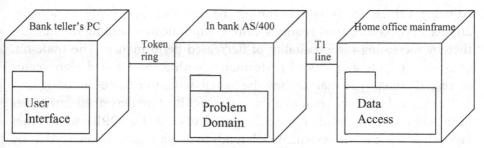

FIGURE 11.7. Deployment diagram.

accepts messages from objects, decides where they need to go, and delivers them to the proper objects. All of this functionality is hidden from the developer. Currently, there are three ORB options:

1. Sun's Java Remote Method Invocation (Java RMI): good for communicating among Java objects on distributed sites;
2. Microsoft's Distributed COM (DCOM): good for communicating among Java and ActiveX objects in a Windows environment; and
3. The Object Management Group's Common Request Broker Architecture (CORBA): a standard to allow any object of any type to communicate across any type of platform; OMG does not sell the necessary CORBA software, but it is provided by several vendors such as IBM and Hewlett-Packard. This is the only truly generic communicating mechanism among the three. It is the only one that allows, for example, Java components to communicate with Smalltalk components.

Which ORB option should be used? For simple Java-only environments, use the Java RMI. For complex or mixed-environments, use CORBA. DCOM is restrictive because it limits the platforms (currently) to only Windows environments, which, of course, defeats one of the primary advantages of Java— portability.

We recommend you visit the Sun, Microsoft, and OMG web sites for more information concerning the Java RMI, DCOM, and CORBA, respectively.

PERFORMANCE ISSUES

OO development and Java both provide great flexibility in software development and execution. Unfortunately, some of these benefits carry a cost.

Utilizing a three-tier design separating the user interface, problem domain, and data access functions requires more communication among the objects, thereby increasing the possibility of decreased performance. The trade-off, of course, is potential loss of performance with a three-tier design versus increased difficulty in maintaining the system without a three-tier design.

Distributed systems, such as a three-tier architecture described earlier, require additional overhead because they need an ORB. The ORB adds another layer of software to the system, which tends to degrade performance. Also, by their nature, distributed systems may have performance problems due to the physical separation of components.

Perhaps the hardest knock on Java to date has been its performance. Some of this is due to the Java environment and the portability it provides. As an interpreted language (using bytecodes and Java virtual machines), performance can suffer. Also, because Java is being widely used in distributed environments, many of which are Internet based, performance has tended to suffer because of communication bottlenecks. The blame cannot be placed solely on Java. Any language in a distributed environment using ORBs may suffer some, it just happens that Java is the language receiving heavy use and attention and thus the criticism that comes with it.

In situations where performance is an important issue, we can use a native language compiler to produce executable Java code, bypass bytecode, and eliminate the JVM. Of course when we do this, we are sacrificing portability.

SUMMARY OF KEY POINTS IN CHAPTER 11

1. OO programming is only one portion of the overall OO development process. Programming cannot stand alone. To develop good OO systems, you must also use OO analysis and design.
2. UML is the standard notation set for object-oriented modeling. It is not a methodology.
3. Several OO development methodologies exist, including the Rational Unified Process and OPEN. Commercial methodologies are also available.
4. In OO analysis, problem domain classes are identified and requirements are modeled using several UML diagrams.
5. In OO design, models created during analysis are enhanced and implementation details, such as interfaces, data access, and technology architecture considerations, are added.

6. Classes should be designed such that the user interface, problem domain, and data access segments are separated (called a three-tiered design). These classes should communicate via messages only.
7. Consideration should be given to the physical placement of objects. The technology architecture, primarily single machine, two-tiered, three-tiered, and *n*-tiered, will impact the placement decisions.
8. Object request brokers (ORBs) are necessary to facilitate communication between objects in a multitiered architecture.
9. There are potential performance problems with Java and OO systems in general due to the multitiered nature of many of the systems and the requisite use of ORBs and three-tiered designs.

BIBLIOGRAPHY

Ambler, S. W. (2001). *Agile Modeling Home Page.* http://www. agilemodeling. com.

Ambler, S.W. (2002). *Agile Modeling: Effective Practices for XP and RUP.* New York: John Wiley.

Arlow, J., and Neustadt, I. (2001). *UML and the Unified Process: Practical Object-Oriented Analysis and Design.* Reading, MA: Addison-Wesley.

Beck, K. (2000). *Extreme Programming Explained – Embrace Change.* Reading, MA: Addison-Wesley Longman.

Beedle, M., and Schwaber, K. (2001). *Agile Software Development with SCRUM.* Upper Saddle River, NJ: Prentice Hall.

Booch, G., Rumbaugh, J., Jacobson, I. (1999). *The Unified Modeling Language User Guide.* Reading, MA: Addison-Wesley.

Chapman, D. (1996). *Understanding ActiveX and OLE: A Guide for Developers & Managers.* Redmond, WA: Microsoft Press.

Graham, I., Henderson-Sellers, B., and Younessi, H. (1999). *The OPEN Process Specification.* Reading, MA: Addison-Wesley.

Krutchen, P. (2003). *The Rational Unified Process: An Introduction,* 3rd Ed. Reading, MA: Addison-Wesley.

Orfali, R., and Harkey, D. (1998). *Client/Server Programming with Java and CORBA,* 2nd Ed. New York: John Wiley.

Glossary

Abstract. A Java keyword used in the class header to indicate the class cannot be used to create objects. Instead, objects are created from a subclass.

Accessor method. A method that returns an attribute value. Named with a prefix "get" plus the variable name.

Aggregation. A relationship among classes wherein one class is a component or part of another class.

Applet. A Java program that runs under the control of a viewer or browser.

Argument. The variable(s) passed to a method.

Assignment operator. An operator used to assign a value to a variable, such as
    =, +=, -=, etc.

Assignment statement. A Java program statement that assigns a value to a variable, such as "double newCost = oldCost*2;". The expression on the right side of the assignment operator (=) is evaluated and the result is placed in the variable on the left of the assignment operator.

Association. A connection (not considered inheritance or aggregation) between two or more classes.

Attribute. What an object knows about itself; an object's data.

Bean (a.k.a. JavaBean). An independent, reusable software component. JavaBeans can be combined to create an application.

Binary association. An association between two classes.

Boolean variable. A variable whose value is either true or false.

Byte stream. A flow of data in Unicode format.

Case structure. A multiple-direction decision structure that can often replace nested `if` statements. Implemented in COBOL with the `EVALUATE` verb and in Java with the `switch` statement.

Casting. The process of changing the data type of a variable in an assignment statement to override a potential truncation error.

Catch. A Java keyword used to intercept an exception that has been thrown.

Character stream. A flow of data in the system's native format, automatically converted back to Unicode when coming into a program.

Class. A group of objects that share common attributes and common behaviors; also, a section of Java program code that contains variables and methods, often used to create objects.

Class header. The first line in a class definition containing class accessibility, class name, and other keywords (such as `public class MyClass{`).

Class method. A static method that provides services for the class and not for a specific object of the class.

Class program. A Java program written to model a class. The program contains the instance variables and instance methods for the class.

Class scope. A variable defined outside all class methods has class scope and is accessible to all methods within the class.

Common Request Broker Architecture (CORBA). An OMG standard that allows any object of any type to communicate across any type of platform.

Compiled code. Machine-readable code, converted from computer language syntax using a compiler.

Complex data type. An object, not one of the eight Java primitive data types (see primitive data type).

Compound condition. Two or more conditions joined with the Java logical operators || (or) or && (and).

Condition. An expression consisting of arithmetic, relational, and/or logical operators that is either true or false.

Condition name. The name of a COBOL condition defined as a level 88.

Conditional operator. A Java coding shortcut to writing simple `if` statements. Its format is: variable = logical expression ? value-1 : value-2;

Constant. A variable defined using the keyword `final`. Its value cannot be changed during program execution.

Constructor method. A method used to create objects. It must have the same name as the class in which it exists.

Custom exception. A class written by the programmer to handle unique situations not handled by standard Java exceptions.

Custom method. A method designed and written to do some custom processing.

Data access classes. The objects and classes that allow storage, retrieval, and manipulation of data.

Data type. The type of data contained in a variable (such as integer, double precision, or string). Java has eight primitive types.

Data type classes. Same as wrapper classes.

Decrement operator. An operator that decrements the value of a variable by 1. A pre-decrement operator (`--i`) acts before the expression containing the variable is evaluated while the post-decrement operator (`i--`) acts only after the expression containing the variable is evaluated.

Deployment diagrams. A diagram that shows the physical location of objects, groups of objects, or portions of objects.

Distributed COM (DCOM). Microsoft's ORB used for communicating among Java and ActiveX objects in a Windows environment.

Dynamic binding. The act of validating classes and methods at runtime, not compile time.

Encapsulation (a.k.a. information hiding). The placement of program implementation details (attributes and behaviors) within an object so they are not directly accessible to other programs, classes, or objects.

Event. A user action involving a GUI component such as clicking a button or selecting a menu item.

Event-driven programming. A programming paradigm where actions occur in response to events.

Event-handler method. The method called to respond to an event.

Event listening. The process by which a listener object listens for events involving a source object (such as a button or menu item) Whenever a source object event occurs, Java calls the appropriate event-handler method `actionPerformed()`.

Event registration. A listener object registers for an event by calling a registration method in the source object. The registration method is

addWindowListener() for Frames and **addActionListener()** for buttons and menu items.

Exception. An object created to deal with a condition. The exception contains information about the condition.

Expression. A combination of variables, literals, and operators that evaluates to a result.

final. A Java keyword used to define variables whose values cannot be changed during program execution.

Hybrid object-oriented language. A language that uses an existing language as its base and adds object-oriented features and syntax.

Identifier. Text used for the name associated with Java programs, classes, methods, and variables.

implements. A Java keyword used in the class header to inherit from another class or interface.

Increment operator. An operator that increments the value of a variable by 1. A preincrement operator (++i) acts before the expression containing the variable is evaluated while the postincrement operator (i++) acts only after the expression containing the variable is evaluated.

Index. A variable containing a value that points to a specific element in a Java array. Java index values begin with 0 for the first element. In a two-dimensional array, the first index refers to the row and the second to the column, relative to zero.

Inheritance. A relationship among classes wherein one class (the subclass) has full access to all attributes and behaviors defined in another class (the superclass).

Instance. Another term for an object.

Instance method. A method that provides services for a specific instance of the class.

Instruction scope. A variable declared within a statement has statement or instruction scope.

Interface. Similar to a class, but with several restrictions.

Java archive files (JAR files). A Java file format used for compressing many files into one to improve transmission speed across network connections.

Java Software Development Kit (Java SDK). Sun's software development environment for writing applets and applications in Java.

Java Integrated Development Environment (Java IDE). A complete Java development environment including compilers, debuggers, interpreters, etc.

Java Virtual Machine (JVM). A Java interpreter; responsible for interpreting bytecodes.

JavaScript. A web scripting language developed by Netscape, which has similar constructs to Java, but is a separate language. JavaScript is typically used for user interface features within HTML documents, but it can also be used on the server side.

Layout manager. Java classes used to place GUI components in a frame or panel.

Listener object. An object that responds to an event.

Logical expression. An expression that evaluates to a boolean value—true or false; a condition.

Logical operator. Java operators used to express logical relationships for "and," "or," and "not" (&&, ||, and !, respectively).

Message. A method call from one object to another, usually consisting of the object's name, a method name, and required parameters.

Method header. The first line of a method definition indicating accessibility, return data type, method name, and parameter list.

Method scope. A variable declared within a method has method scope. It is accessible only within the method.

Method signature. The method name and its parameter list.

Methods. The things an object can do; its behavior.

Multiple inheritance. A subclass (child) with more than one superclass (parent).

Multiplicity. An indication of the number of objects of a class involved in a relationship.

Mutator method. A method that changes the contents of an attribute. Named with the prefix "set" plus the variable name.

n-ary association. An association involving n classes (usually more than three).

Object. A software entity containing both data (what it knows about itself) and behavior (what it can do); it encapsulates attributes and the behaviors designed to change the values of those attributes; a specific member of a class.

Object-based language. A programming language that supports some OO concepts but does not support inheritance.

Object interface. What others outside the object see of the object; usually the object name, method name, and required parameters.

Object name (a.k.a., object pointer). A unique identifier for a specific object.

Object-oriented language. A programming language that supports all OO concepts including inheritance.

Object persistence. The technique of storing objects, or their attribute values, so they may be reconstructed at a later time.

Object reference variable. A variable that refers to or points to an object.

Object request broker (ORB). An entity that keeps track of object locations and provides the communication mechanisms to allow objects to communicate.

Object serialization. A Java technique introduced with JDK 1.1 used to store complete objects in a file. These objects can be retrieved intact as if they were just created.

One-dimensional array. An array that has only one dimension, a row of elements. A Java array is really an object and is referenced with an object reference variable.

OPEN. Object-Oriented Process, Environment, and Notation; an object-oriented methodology developed by a consortium of 32 members; utilizes UML and other notation sets.

Package. A Java class library.

Package diagrams. Elements that provide a logical grouping of classes.

Panel. An invisible GUI component used to contain other components.

Parameter. The variables received by a method.

Passing by reference. Passing a reference variable as an argument to a method is called passing by reference because we pass a reference to the data instead of a copy of the data. Note that when a method receives a reference variable, it has access to the object referenced by the variable.

Persistent object. An object that exists longer than the execution of the program.

Polymorphism. The condition that exists when the same message can elicit a different response, depending on the receiver of the message.

Portability. The ability to run an application on different platforms without making changes to the code.

Post-test loop. A loop whose terminating condition is tested at the end of the loop.

Pre-test loop. A loop whose terminating condition is tested at the beginning of the loop.

Primitive data type. One of the eight basic types of data in Java (int, short, long, byte, float, double, char, and boolean).

Private access. Only this program has access to this method or variable.

Problem domain classes. The objects and classes representing business logic.

Public access. Any program has access to this method or variable.

Pure object-oriented language. A language in which everything is represented as an object and all major characteristics of object-orientation such as inheritance, classes, and polymorphism are supported.

Reference variable. A variable that points to an object.

Relational operator. Java operators used in writing logical expressions (<, >, <=, >=, ==, &&, ||, !, !=).

Remote Method Invocation (RMI). A Sun Microsystems ORB; good for communicating among Java objects on distributed sites.

Restricted access. Only this program and its subclasses have access to this method or variable.

Return. A Java statement that returns a specified variable to the calling program.

Scope. The accessibility of a variable. Java variables have class, method, or instruction scope.

Sequence diagrams. Elements that illustrate the timing and sequence of messages between classes and objects.

Servlet. Similar to an applet, but is located on the server; provides added functionality to Java-enabled servers.

Single inheritance. A subclass (child) with only one superclass (parent).

Socket. An object of the Socket class; used to establish communication between a client and a server.

Source object. The object where an event originates, generally a button or menu item.

SQL. Structured Query Language; a standardized (ANSI) database language. Java uses classes in the java.sql package to execute SQL statements.

Static binding. The act of validating all classes and methods at compile time.

Static. A Java keyword meaning only one copy is to exist. Static variables are sometimes called class variables.

Static method. A class method that provides services for the class, but not for a specific object of the class.

Stream. A flow of data either into or out of a program.

String. A supplied Java class whose objects contain character string data. These objects are complex data type.

Subclass (a.k.a. child). A class that inherits attributes and/or methods from another class.

Subscript. A COBOL term corresponding to a Java index. It points to an element in an array.

Superclass (a.k.a. parent). A class whose attributes and behaviors are inherited from by other classes.

Systems development methodology (SDM). A detailed guide for the development of a system; a "how to" book for developing systems.

Ternary association. An association involving three classes.

`this`. A Java keyword that refers to the current object of the class.

Three-tier design. System design where the user interface, problem domain, and data access segments are separated.

Throw an exception. The process of sending an exception object is called throwing and uses the keyword `throw`.

Transient object. An object that is erased from memory when the program terminates.

Two-dimensional array. An array that has only two dimensions, elements arranged into rows and columns. A Java array is really an instance and is referenced with an instance reference variable.

Type casting. The act of changing the data type of a variable.

UML. Unified Modeling Language; the standard object modeling notation adopted by the Object Management Group.

Unary association. An association involving only one class.

Unicode. A standard character set used by Java. Each Unicode character requires 2 bytes.

Unified process (UP). An object-oriented software development methodology that (a) utilizes UML and (b) is published by Rational Corporation.

User interface classes. The objects and classes that allow the user to interact with the system.

Variable. A place in memory used to store data. The data can be either a value or a pointer to an object.

Wrapper classes. Java classes for each of the primitive data types.

Index

Printed in the United States
by Baker & Taylor Publisher Services